'Reinhard Stelter has lead the way in thinking about coaching as a humanistic developmental methodology. This book crystallises his latest thinking and will be invaluable to coaches, consultants and everyone who has an interest in developmental approaches to coaching. A must read.'
– **Professor Anthony M. Grant**, Director, Coaching Psychology Unit, University of Sydney, Australia

'As the world becomes more complex and the pace of our lives accelerates, deep personal reflection and social connection become ever more essential. Reinhard's enlightening book lays out a path to connect both elements in a rich, shared dialogue. Those who embrace this approach will begin a profoundly transformational journey.'
– **David B. Peterson, PhD**; Director, Center of Expertise, Executive Coaching & Leadership Development, Google, Inc.

'This is a lovely, readable, and important book. Professor Stelter's command of the thought of thinkers such as Buber, Gendlin, and Kierkegaard is exemplary as is his synthesis of philosophical and psychological theory with the field of coaching practice. He is mindful of the chaotic social and cultural context in which we live and brings to it a deeply humanistic and insightful perspective on how meaningful dialogue can help those who are coached. Dialogue, he argues, can help people find grounding within themselves even as they deal with the flux and demands that surround them. This book will be appreciated by anyone who wants to better understand the art and practice of conversation.'
– **Steen Halling**, Professor Emeritus of Psychology, Seattle University, USA; author of *Intimacy, Transcendence, and Psychology*

'This book is a compelling argument for the type of coaching that needs to respond to the disturbing dynamics of the industrialised world. Although I hope that some strands of coaching or some individual coaches are already working with this level of challenge, Reinhard Stelter's proposition crystallises their intentions into a coherent approach. This deeply thoughtful and passionate book is essential for coaching education and important for all professionals who wish coaching to be a tangible contribution to the state of the world.'
– **Professor Tatiana Bachkirova**, Director of the International Centre for Coaching and Mentoring Studies, Oxford Brookes University, UK

The Art of Dialogue in Coaching

In *The Art of Dialogue in Coaching*, Reinhard Stelter invites readers to engage in transformative and fruitful dialogues in everyday working life, and provides the theory and tools for them to be able to do so.

Presented in three parts, the book provides a complete overview of the importance of dialogue and how it can be utilised. Part I, Theoretical basis, examines third-generation coaching as a collaborative dialogue form, the societal context of the coaching process and the concept of identity in modern society. Part II, Basic themes of fruitful dialogue, examines meaning-making, value and the narrative perspective, and their significance in creating a new dialogue culture. Finally, Part III, Reflections on dialogue practice, explores the art of being a supporting dialogue guide, drawing on a number of theoretical perspectives and focusing on developing relational competencies. Stelter emphasises that taking the time to linger opens new possibilities for fundamental self-insight, and clearly explains how dialogue provides us with a framework for acting in the world with personal integrity.

The Art of Dialogue in Coaching will be an essential guide for coaches in practice and in training, coaching psychologists and professionals with a coaching role, including mentors, consultants and leaders. In particular, it will appeal to those looking to conduct dialogue as an art form, enhancing their work as a co-creative and collaborative guide.

Reinhard Stelter, **PhD**, is a professor of coaching psychology and head of the Coaching Psychology Unit at NEXS, University of Copenhagen, and visiting professor at Copenhagen Business School, Denmark. He is honorary vice president and Associate Fellow of the International Society of Coaching Psychology, and a coaching practitioner, researcher, lecturer, workshop leader and facilitator in private practice.

Coaching Psychology
Series Editor: Stephen Palmer

Coaching psychology is a distinct branch of academic and applied psychology that focuses on enhancement of performance, development and wellbeing in the broader population. Written by leading experts, the **Coaching Psychology** series will highlight innovations in the field, linking theory, research and practice. These books will interest professionals from psychology, coaching, mentoring, business, health, human resources and management as well as those interested in the psychology underpinning their coaching and mentoring practice.

www.routledge.com/Coaching-Psychology/book-series/COACHPSYCH

Titles in the series:

Coaching Psychology in Schools
Enhancing Performance, Development and Wellbeing
Mark Adams

Very Brief Cognitive Behavioural Coaching (VBCBC)
Windy Dryden

Coaching Psychology for Learning
Facilitating Growth in Education
Qing Wang

Positive Psychology Coaching in Practice
Suzy Green and Stephen Palmer

The Art of Dialogue in Coaching
Towards Transformative Exchange
Reinhard Stelter

The Art of Dialogue in Coaching

Towards Transformative Change

Reinhard Stelter

LONDON AND NEW YORK

First published 2019
by Routledge
2 Park Square, Milton Park, Abingdon, Oxon, OX14 4RN

and by Routledge
711 Third Avenue, New York, NY 10017

Routledge is an imprint of the Taylor & Francis Group, an informa business

© 2019 Taylor & Francis

The right of Reinhard Stelter to be identified as author of this work has been asserted by him in accordance with sections 77 and 78 of the Copyright, Designs and Patents Act 1988.

All rights reserved. No part of this book may be reprinted or reproduced or utilised in any form or by any electronic, mechanical, or other means, now known or hereafter invented, including photocopying and recording, or in any information storage or retrieval system, without permission in writing from the publishers.

Trademark notice: Product or corporate names may be trademarks or registered trademarks, and are used only for identification and explanation without intent to infringe.

Library of Congress Cataloging-in-Publication Data
Names: Stelter, Reinhard, 1954- author.

Title: The art of dialogue in coaching : towards transformative change / Reinhard Stelter.
Description: New York, NY : Routledge, 2019. |
Series: Coaching psychology |
Includes bibliographical references and index.
Identifiers: LCCN 2018025586 (print) | LCCN 2018027973 (ebook) | ISBN 9781351006538 (Adobe Reader) | ISBN 9781351006521 (ePub) | ISBN 9781351006514 (Mobipocket) | ISBN 9781351006545 (Master Ebook) | ISBN 9781138543553 (pbk.) | ISBN 9781351006545 (ebook) | ISBN 9781138543546 (hardback)
Subjects: LCSH: Counseling psychology. | Personal coaching.
Classification: LCC BF636.6 (ebook) | LCC BF636.6 .S74 2019 (print) | DDC 158.3—dc23
LC record available at https://lccn.loc.gov/2018025586

ISBN: 978-1-138-54354-6 (hbk)
ISBN: 978-1-138-54355-3 (pbk)
ISBN: 978-1-351-00654-5 (ebk)

Typeset in Times New Roman
by Florence Production Ltd, Stoodleigh, Devon, UK

Contents

Preface vii
Acknowledgements x

PART I
Theoretical basis 1

1 Third-generation coaching as sustainable, fruitful dialogue: Key navigation points 3
2 The societal context: the emergence of the achievement-subject and the burnout society 15
3 Searching for one's own self: identity as one of the key challenges of our time 23

PART II
Basic themes of fruitful dialogues 39

4 Meaning-making in dialogue 41
5 Values – a basis for action 57
6 The narrative perspective: transformation through sharing 71

PART III
Reflections on dialogue practice 79

7 Enhancing attention 81
8 The narrative co-creative practice 97

9 The foundation of dialogue and the dialogue guide's virtues	111
10 Dialogue practices	123
Concluding reflections	135
References	137
Index of names	145
Index	147

Preface

At the time of writing, four years have passed since my book *A Guide to Third Generation Coaching: Narrative-Collaborative Theory and Practice* was published by Springer (the English edition of the original edition in Danish). Over the years, I have held a large number of courses, workshops, presentations and lectures in Denmark and abroad for students, fellow researchers, executives, consultants, psychologists, coaches and practitioners of reflective dialogues wishing to enhance their understanding of and skill in leading open, fruitful and transformative dialogues.

Many readers have told me how much they welcome the book and its innovative approach to coaching. There is considerable interest in third-generation coaching, and the approach is now in use in a wide range of practice fields. Since *A Guide to Third Generation Coaching* was published in 2014 I have gained additional experience with the method as a coach and dialogue guide. I have also conducted a number of research projects and supervised several PhD studies that explicitly incorporate third-generation coaching. In the present book I aim to share these experiences with you in a variety of ways. I use third-generation coaching as the underlying inspiration for a range of different dialogue forms and offer reflections on the approach and on society at large, coaching theories and dialogue practices.

I should point out that it has never been my intention to focus exclusively on the third-generation level. That is hardly possible. Thus, I incorporate perspectives from the first two generations of coaching: coaching with a problem and goal perspective (first generation) and coaching that applies a strength perspective aimed at addressing possible solutions and future scenarios, with inspiration from systemic and social-constructionist approaches (second generation). Regardless of the approach, however, any good coach and dialogue guide who keeps the focus person's current social and societal challenges in mind should strive to enhance the perspective of third-generation coaching by maintaining a particular emphasis on values and narrative co-creation and by minimizing the emphasis on goals and performance optimization.

The impetus for the present book

A Guide to Third Generation Coaching has been an ambitious, research-based and fairly comprehensive textbook that some readers may find a bit overwhelming. I therefore welcome Routledge's interest in publishing a new and very different book on the topic that broadens the concepts of third-generation coaching, highlighting and developing the particular aspects of a dialogue form that aims to heighten awareness of pitfalls and challenges for coaches and other dialogue guides working in our current societal climate.

This book widens the horizon of my earlier work, as it underscores a certain *current need*: the need for an *ability to take the time to linger* – an ability that we are losing, and which needs to be revitalized. On the other hand, it is also an independent publication with new thoughts and ideas that have not previously been published. The book will therefore be of interest both to new readers and to readers and practitioners who are familiar with *A Guide to Third Generation Coaching* and have maintained their curiosity about a further development of the approach.

The ambition and purpose of the book

I am so pleased that I have been given this opportunity to present my ideas in a new book that is not 'merely' the essence of my earlier work, but a great opportunity for me to disseminate the development of my research and thinking over the past 20 years. My main ambition is to invite you, the reader, to engage in *transformative and fruitful dialogues* in your everyday working life. Hence, my focus will not be exclusively on coaching as a particular professional dialogue format that should only be practiced by specially trained dialogue guides.

My hope is to incorporate third-generation coaching in a search for a dialogue form that is applicable in many life contexts. The dialogue partner (the 'coachee' or 'focus person') is liberated by being invited to discover his or her ethical stance and the personal values that make everyday life meaningful. Pausing and lingering in the dialogue opens new possibilities for fundamental self-insight. The dialogue provides us with a framework for acting in the world with personal integrity. Thus, the dialogue is not a quick fix, but a *sustainable conversation* that helps a person discover where they stand.

I therefore invite anyone who is interested in helping others develop greater self-insight to read this book. In the book I distinguish between the roles of *dialogue guide* and *dialogue partner*. The *dialogue guide* is the person who aims to provide help through the dialogue. This person is a professional – coach, mentor, psychologist, consultant, support person or leader – or a good friend or co-worker who is willing to take on the role as dialogue guide, based on an explicit agreement. The *dialogue partner* is the person who requests help in the form of this particular form of dialogue. It is important that the two parties define their respective positions in the conversation and a set of ground rules ahead of time. Thus, the intended audience includes anyone who wishes to improve their skills as co-creative and collaborative dialogue guides who do their best to conduct dialogue as an art form – the art of lingering in dialogue.

Copenhagen, July 2018

Acknowledgements

On this occasion I would like to thank the many trainees, workshop participants, coachees, colleagues and PhD and graduate students whose reflections and collaboration have helped me enhance my focus on dialogues that are inspired and framed by third-generation coaching. I have benefited tremendously from my longstanding cooperation with Professor Ole Fogh Kirkeby of the Copenhagen Business School through our involvement in the Master of Public Governance programme and with former Associate Professor and Kierkegaard scholar Pia Søltoft in connection with our joint courses at the Copenhagen Summer University, which has contributed profoundly to my constant interest in phenomenological and existential issues. In addition, I would like to acknowledge Professor Bo Jacobsen, who has at times provided professional supervision to me; my three colleagues from the Taos Institute (where I am an associate): Kenneth Gergen, Sheila McNamee and John Shotter (who sadly passed away in 2017); and my colleagues for many years from the Copenhagen Coaching Center, especially Mette Mejlhede and Andreas Bering. I am grateful to my beloved wife Shereen Horami, who has supported me both in her role as psychologist and as my companion in life. Together with her I feel inspired and cheerful.

Furthermore, I would like to thank my many international colleagues and friends, who all supported me in enhancing my understanding of coaching and transformative dialogues during the many years of our cooperation: Stephen Palmer, Uwe Böning, Siegfried Greif, Robert Wegener, Antony Grant, Michael Cavanagh, Tatiana Bachkirova, David Drake, David Lane, Ho Law, Jonathan Passmore, Chené Swart, Alleta Odendal, Carol Kauffman, Lew Stern, Sandy Gordon, Ole Michael Spaten, Tobias Dam, Silvana Dini, Samuel Silvestre Antunes and many others. – I am grateful for your support.

A big thanks goes to my two Danish reviewers, MA (psych.) Vibe Strøier, who is a specialist in psychotherapy and organizational psychology, and Professor Ole Fogh Kirkeby, and to the former editor Birgitte Lie Suhr-Jessen of Dansk Psykologisk Forlag. Their contributions have been invaluable for the form and quality of the book. I am grateful for the amazing work of my translator, Dorte H. Silver. You have given me a voice in English where I would have felt limited in expressing myself.

Finally, I would like to thank my colleagues and department heads for the opportunities I am granted to engage in research, teaching and communication that lets me explore coaching and coaching psychology and its many facets. I am fortunate to have a workplace that gives me every opportunity to develop and grow on both a personal and professional level – in autumn 2015, through my research stay at the University of Western Australia, where this work began, and where I had more time than I do in my everyday work to explore – and linger on and in – my thinking. I look forward to new opportunities to work with new partners who share my passion for coaching, leadership and development.

I wish you a good time reading, lots of inspiration and many fruitful dialogues!

www.rstelter.dk and www.nexs.ku.dk/coaching

Part I

Theoretical basis

2 Theoretical basis

In the following three chapters I seek to develop a basic understanding of what is going on in society and of the potential role of third-generation coaching and other sustainable, fruitful and transformative dialogues for the individual and for our personal and professional interactions. Transformative dialogues are conversations that develop our identity. The purpose of these dialogues is to challenge the self-perception, worldview and values of the dialogue partner (or partners) looking for help. Transformative dialogues are sustainable and fruitful because they provide a basis for improving the person's long-term ability to handle the major challenges presented by today's society.

The following three chapters outline a theoretical basis for understanding the special role of dialogue in relation to societal changes and their impact on individual identity development:

In **Chapter 1** I outline the fundamentals of third-generation coaching as a specific dialogue form. In this chapter I also address the justified criticism that has been directed at certain types of coaching over the years. Not all conversations and dialogue forms will be helpful for a given person. It is important to understand both the social and the organizational context of the conversation. Coaching should be viewed as a way to lead fruitful and transformative dialogues.

In **Chapter 2** I examine the societal context of the coaching process. We live in a burnout society where stress is fast becoming the most prevalent cause of sick leave. In this context it is important to build a dialogue culture that breaks with the prevailing agenda of expecting people to take on ever-greater workloads and live up to growing performance requirements. Third-generation coaching is intended as a fruitful and transformative dialogue that aims to reintroduce the art of lingering in the moment.

In **Chapter 3** I address the concept of identity as a key topic in today's society. The conditions of the modern world have shaken us to our core. The need to deal with the constant flow of information and to navigate in a network of social relations makes it ever harder for us to prioritize. The dream of living an authentic life often has to remain just that, a dream, due to the power discourse that determines our social behaviour. The concept of *heteroenticity* – the ability to relate to oneself through the other – is introduced as a means of leading sustainable, fruitful and transformative dialogues.

Chapter 1

Third-generation coaching as sustainable, fruitful dialogue
Key navigation points

In this chapter I address some current positions that reflect a critical view of coaching. I elaborate on the coaching concept and clarify the necessary reorientation towards coaching as an open, fruitful and transformative dialogue. With this, I address justified points of criticism by presenting third-generation coaching as a dialogue format that offers an innovative option for people who need to find themselves as a crucial condition for being able to survive the pressures we face, as individuals, in today's society. I outline the key characteristics of third-generation coaching, define and describe its purpose and lay out the foundation for an understanding of coaching as a special form of co-creative dialogue.

Experience with third-generation coaching and relevant points of criticism

Throughout my many years of work with coaching I have increasingly realized how important it is for the coach to be *a fellow human being* and *a co-creative partner* in the dialogue. Coaching should not be limited to a performance-oriented and goal-driven agenda. An ethically sound dialogue framework has to be shaped in accordance with the dialogue partner's own agenda and readiness. In a world where we are leading increasingly isolated lives, and where we are often left to fend for ourselves to meet the demands we face, it is crucial that we establish a meaningful counterweight in the form of analogue social venues and communities with room for fruitful conversation – where no one feels that they have to say something in order to earn 'likes'. We need to rediscover the art of lingering in dialogue.

My main ambition with this book is to present coaching as a *sustainable dialogue form*. The term 'sustainable' was carefully chosen, and in this context it carries the following meaning: ultimately, the dialogue partner (the coachee or focus person) should be liberated from the dialogue guide (the coach) by *discovering his or her standpoint and rootedness* in a set of personal values. The dialogue should always support the individual's search for personal meaning and thus promote a framework and an integrity that help the person 'be him/herself', 'find him/herself' or – to quote Kierkegaard – 'choose himself'.[1] Naturally, however, this individual quest should always unfold in interaction with others. At a time when individuals are increasingly losing control over their own lives and lacking a sense of being rooted in stable and enduring social relationships, interpersonal dialogues should serve to enhance the individual's identity and self-concept – given the awareness that *the self* does not exist as a stable core self but develops in the contexts of our social engagements with others and in the dynamics of our relationships.

My colleague Svend Brinkmann pursues a similar ambition in his much-debated book *Stand Firm*, published in 2017. He too is an advocate of allowing people to *be themselves and find themselves*. Brinkmann's ideas have provoked both uncertainty and anger among professional therapists, coaches and mindfulness instructors. He even proposed seven guidelines for life, one of which was 'Sack your coach!'.[2] The ensuing debate clearly showed that many misunderstood Brinkmann's agenda, which takes aim squarely at today's prevailing demand for people to embrace permanent change. Brinkmann lends a hand to people who are willing to do anything to keep up with development and who are thus at risk of burning out. He offers an alternative. And he has a point! As long as coaches offer to help their clients pursue the ill-conceived desire to 'keep up' at all costs, they should be sacked. Such a narrow focus on goals and performance is not helpful. We need to rediscover the art of lingering in dialogue – for our own sake and for the sake of those around us!

Dialogue as shared meaning-making

The agenda of third-generation coaching[3] is to offer a space for reflection where the coach and the focus person together can search for the meaning of life or find meaning in certain events or situations that the focus person is involved in. In many cases, the answer does not lie within the individual him/herself, but in the relationship – in the interaction and dialogue between two people or, in group coaching, in the larger group. In a comment acknowledging the merits of Brinkmann's book, I have been quoted as follows:

> Sometimes one needs to return to oneself, engaging in a reflection process in order to find out who one is. So, coaching has a new agenda now. It is not only

---

1 In *Either/Or* from 1843 Kierkegaard describes the ethical challenge as a crucial task for a human being: choosing oneself means taking responsibility for oneself, embracing one's history and thus also living with the opportunities and limitations that life has to offer (see: http://sks.dk/EE1/txt.xml).
2 www.psychologytoday.com/blog/stand-firm/201702/how-stand-firm-in-runaway-world [retrieved on 13 Feb. 2018].
3 Grant (2017) introduced the term 'third "generation" of workplace coaching', which has a different meaning and should not be seen as similar to the use of the term here.

supposed to move people, it should also tell them where they are, in order to give them a sense of certainty and a basic understanding of themselves.[4]

It is in dialogues, in interactions with another or others, that we become who we are. Martin Buber[5] wrote: 'Through the *Thou* a man becomes *I*'. In a society that is increasingly individualized, where people often struggle alone to survive, we need to develop solidarity and a form of dialogue that strengthens both or all interlocutors.

First-generation coaching has its roots in sport. Its focus is on goals and problems. Second-generation coaching revolves around possible solutions and appreciative dialogues and is rooted in systemic and social-constructionist theory.[6] These coaching approaches still offer much that we can use today. Times have changed, however, and we need to rethink coaching fundamentally. That is even happening in the world of sport, where the focus is shifting away from an exclusive emphasis on results and towards shaping development and strong performances in a good environment, in cooperation with coaches with insight into human nature.[7] Coaching with an exclusive focus on specific goals that aims to solve individual problems by boosting the person's skills and performance capacity may result in a sense of inadequacy and, ultimately, in stress and despair. Workplace performance standards – our own and others' – can sometimes seem inhumane and overwhelming. The individualization of complex issues in the workplace that is often a part of traditional coaching promotes *'dangerous leadership'*.[8] With its focus on specific personal goals first-generation coaching, in particular, is unsuited as a dialogue form for leaders or managers in relation to their staff. With reference to Ole Fogh Kirkeby I have always warned against leaders abusing coaching as a form of intimate technology.[9] Second-generation coaching also perpetuates the concept of untapped resources in dialogue partner that need to be mobilized. The co-creative perspective is missing. In the first two generations of coaching, the coach is a more or less neutral dialogue facilitator. In third-generation coaching, the coach becomes an engaged fellow human companion. That is the only way for human beings to meet in a shared space based on empathy and solidarity.

I invite you, the reader, to share a dream with me of *leading dialogues that enrich both parties*. Naturally, one of the parties, often referred to as 'the coach', has

---

4 The popular Danish research website: http://videnskab.dk/kultur-samfund/fa-et-bedre-liv-vend-selvhjaelpsbogernes-budskaber-pa-hovedet
5 Buber, M. (1997). *I and Thou*. Charles Scribner's Sons. 1937. Reprint Continuum International Publishing Group, 2004. (Original German edition: 1923).
6 A more in-depth description of the three coaching generations can be found in Stelter, 2014, pp. 51–53.
7 See, e.g.: *Træneren som Coach* by Jakob Hansen and Kristoffer Henriksen, Dansk Psykologisk Forlag, 2009; or see Mark Nesti's work at Liverpool John Moores University.
8 Cf. Ørsted, C (2013). *Livsfarlig Ledelse*. Copenhagen: People's Press. The book warns against the use of coaching in relation to leadership and management.
9 Cf. Kirkeby, O. F. (2006). 'Coaching: For madonnaer eller ludere?' *LPF-nyt om Ledelse*, 9(2), 10–11.

6 Theoretical basis

a special responsibility for driving the dialogue forward – a professional responsibility to be a good dialogue guide. The coach should also be willing to empathize with the dialogue partner's life world by showing understanding, acceptance and empathy. The coach can provide direction for the conversation and ensure progress by entering his or her own experiences into the dialogue, engaging as a fellow human being by attuning with and providing feedback to the dialogue partner.

In Figures 1.1 and 1.2 I attempt to outline the differences between three different dialogue forms. Figure 1.1 describes the difference between an every-day conversation *about something* and a coaching conversation based on first- or second-generation coaching. Figure 1.2 presents third-generation coaching as a basis for transformative, fruitful and genuine dialogues (the concept of a 'genuine' dialogue refers to the dialogue philosopher Martin Buber; he describes the dialogue as a meeting between two human beings aimed at inviting oneself and the other into a conversation on a deep, existential level). Many coaching conversations will rely on an interactive mix of the three generations of coaching with the purpose of promoting one's third-generation coaching ambition. The two figures may help coaches and other dialogue guides become more aware of their intention in a given conversation. When I speak of transformative, fruitful and genuine dialogues, the ambition is clearly related to the dialogue structure outlined in Figure 1.2.

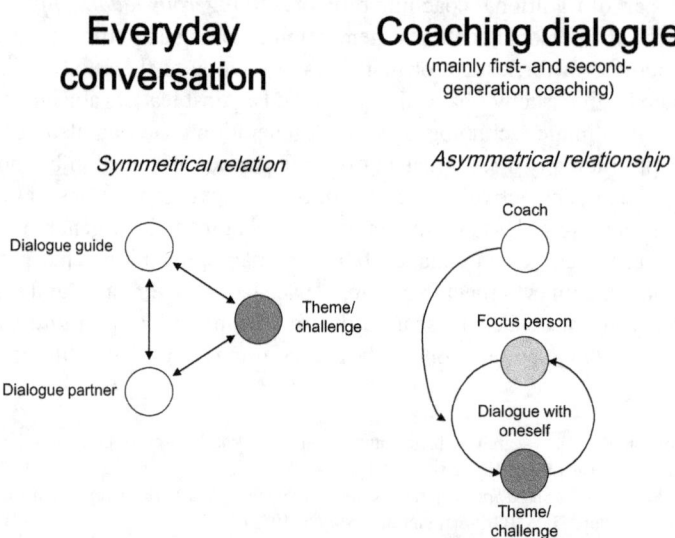

Figure 1.1 Differences between a standard everyday conversation and a first- and second-generation coaching conversation. The symmetry or asymmetry lies in the dialogue guide's own engagement in the topic and the challenge: in the everyday conversation both parties ideally have an equal investment in the topic. This means that the conversation is symmetrical. A first- or second-generation coach acts mainly as a facilitator on behalf of the focus person. That leads to asymmetry, because the coach is not engaged in the topic or the challenge but merely helps the focus person arrive at a solution.

Third-generation coaching
– aiming for transformative, generative and genuine dialogues

*Mainly asymmetrical relationship,
periodically symmetrical*

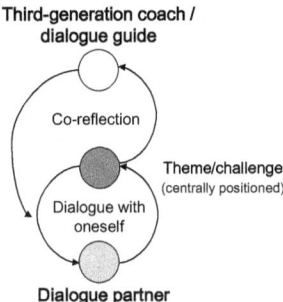

- The dialogue guide supports the dialogue partner's own reflections

- The dialogue guide is an outsider witness and co-reflecting partner in the dialogue

- The dialogue guide is a co-creative fellow human companion in the dialogue

Figure 1.2 Third-generation coaching with a growing ambition of achieving moments of symmetry. Schematically, this is illustrated by the topic or the challenge moving to the centre. Co-reflection becomes a key ambition for the dialogue guide.

My coaching research adventure

Over the past five years (2013–2018) I have had the great pleasure of heading a research project[10] where 24 volunteer coaches,[11] many of them with many years of experience, each served as a coach and mentor to a group of young boys, mainly with an ethnic-minority background. The project lasted two years, with conversations every two or three weeks. The purpose of the project was to challenge the young people to work with the themes of 'life skills', resilience and active citizenship to give them an active experience of being able to manage themselves and others in the arenas of their everyday life.

My own involvement as a coach, together with a female co-coach – who was fully accepted by the boys – was a very rewarding experience. I got to know a group of five boys whom I would not otherwise have met or become acquainted with. Many people in society are suspicious or wary of these 14–15-year-old boys. In the early stages of the project, when the boys asked me, 'Why are you here? What's this about?' I said, 'I would like to get to know you better. If I ran into you guys late one night, I might cross over to the other side of the street. Now I have a chance to

---

10 See more at www.teamsport-health.ku.dk/research/project4/ [retrieved on 13 Feb. 2018].
11 See: https://www.holdspil.ku.dk/forskning/forskningsprojekter/projekt4/frivillige-coaches/ – the project was operated by Copenhagen Centre for Team Sport and Health, which was supported by the private foundation Nordea Fonden.

get to know you properly – and I'm looking forward to it'. With this invitation I created a sense of equality, which is an important base element in third-generation coaching. I did not meet them as a therapist or with a fixed agenda. I showed an interest in them, and I disclosed my own insecurity and my desire to learn.

In hindsight I appreciate how much everyone enjoyed the process.[12] I got to know the boys in a way that would never have been possible otherwise. And the boys, in turn, appreciated me and my interest in them. As their trust in me grew, they began to call me bro', *habibi* or *shabab*. Although guiding them and the conversation was not always an easy task, the boys saw our dialogues as a good opportunity to speak of important issues. I got close enough to them that I agreed to smoking a pipe with them in the local Aladdin Club. They were aware that the focus was on them, as individuals and as a group. All the conversations dealt with their relationship with peers, teachers, family, friends, culture, religion and the Danes, the latter being a group that formally includes them too, but maybe not quite. They were given the time to articulate things that they probably never considered or attended to in depth. In this forum, they said things to each other that made them grow on a personal level. They began to experience a sense of community that empowered them to address each other, also outside the shared space of the coaching conversations. The talks became a meeting place for all of us, and in certain moments they formed an ideal setting for the underlying concept of third-generation coaching.[13]

The key characteristic of fruitful dialogues

I describe third-generation coaching conversations as *fruitful dialogues*. A parallel term that is often used is 'generative dialogues', which characterize a dialogue that is not based on arguments and counterarguments, but on mutually appreciative curiosity, where both (all) parties suspend their pre-existing judgements, assessments and perceptions of each other in an effort to understand and support each other in the common desire to see oneself, the world and each other more clearly. My unique conversations with the boys contained certain ideal aspects of third-generation coaching and fruitful conversations, which I briefly discuss in the following.[14]

---

12 See article in the journal *Folkeskolen*: www.folkeskolen.dk/557883/naar-laererne-blander-sig-udenom-vokser-drengene [The journal for teachers in the primary and lower secondary school; retrieved on 13 Feb. 2018].
13 See also: Ryom, K. E., Maar Andersen, M., & Stelter, R. (2017). Coaching at-risk youth in a school within a socially challenging environment. *Improving Schools*, 20(2), 143–160. DOI: 10.1177/1365480217694955.
14 The basic idea underlying dialogue theory stems from Bohm, D. (1996). *On Dialogue*. New York: Routledge. In a therapeutic context some of these elements are addressed and elaborated in Duncan, B. L., Miller, S. D., Wampold, B. E. & Hubble, M. A. (eds.) (2010). *The Heart & Soul of Change* (2nd edition). Washington, DC: American Psychological Association.

1. The dialogue becomes a meeting place

The optimal point of departure for third-generation coaching conversations and fruitful dialogues is to create a shared meeting place around a topic that is important to both parties. In a coaching conversation, the focus person naturally often brings in a topic, a challenge, a problem or a situation that he or she wishes to discuss – in many cases because the situation presents a problem. In my talks with the boys, I was often the one to introduce a topic that I thought it would be worthwhile to discuss, often driven by my own curiosity or puzzlement. Fundamentally, both parties in the conversation are entitled to shape the direction of the dialogue, either at the outset or during the process. That adds a dynamic to the conversation that was lacking in previous generations of coaching because the coach was required to remain a neutral facilitator based on the challenge brought up by the focus person.[15]

2. The dialogue becomes a journey of discovery

Coaching is at times a journey into uncharted territory, where neither party knows the destination or the route. Both parties – the coach and the focus person – are each other's companions on this journey, and none know the destination at the outset. Their journey is based on a desire and an agreement that something must and will happen. The focus person often comes in with a vision of and a need for new discoveries, a change of course or new perspectives on his or her life. The coach does not provide a road map but acts as an empathic and professionally qualities companion and partner on this journey. In this sense, the dialogue reflects a journey into the unknown, which both parties shape in cooperation, but framed by a fairly safe setting and by an ambition of a satisfactory and life-affirming outcome.

3. The coach/dialogue guide's engagement and professional background are crucial

In our research project, as mentioned above, it was crucial for the coach to be present as a fully engaged dialogue guide. Sometimes, the coach or other members of the group will provide feedback to the statements made in the dialogue. This is where the appreciative perspective takes form. As a dialogue guide the coach acts as a withness-thinking and responsible dialogue partner who relates to what the other says. In narrative thinking, this is called witnessing.[16] Here, a dialogue guide

---

15 Classic systemic coaching emphasizes the need for the coach to remain neutral. See, e.g., my first book on coaching: Stelter, R. (2002). *Coaching – Læring og Udvikling*. Virum: Dansk Psykologisk Forlag.
16 See White, M. (2007). *Maps of Narrative Practice*. New York, NY: Norton; Carey, M. & Russell, S. (2003). Outsider-witness practices: some answers to commonly asked questions. *The International*

– often the coach – reflects what the other said, not in the form of an assessment but as an appreciative and caring curiosity and wondering. The coach becomes a co-reflecting partner in the dialogue, along with any additional group members.

4. The focus person's interest in and commitment to the conversation is supported

In a group setting it is crucial to make active and fruitful contributions to the conversation. Assessments of others should be avoided; instead the aim should be to understand others' unique characteristics as different from one's own; this may ultimately contribute to one's own self-insight. In a therapy context researchers have found that the client's commitment and willingness to develop and change his or her own situation is a key condition for a satisfactory treatment outcome.[17] Thus, the focus person and any other group members can make active and fruitful contributions to the development of the conversation. Here it is important to invite the participants' feedback on whether the conversation – the journey of discovery – is moving in a desired direction. If they have any new ideas or requests, these should be addressed.

5. The dialogue participants form an alliance

In a therapy context, the alliance between the parties is viewed as a key factor for moving the conversation in a fruitful and healing direction. In the research project mentioned above, such an alliance clearly developed in my relationship with the boys. The parties are able to co-create a new reality that is rewarding for everyone involved. This trust, confidence and openness constitute fertile ground for creativity and innovation. Intensity in the conversation and the dialogue participants' mutual appreciation and acknowledgement of each other are crucial indicators of fruitful dialogues.

6. The dialogue is an opportunity for learning

Third-generation coaching and fruitful conversations generally offer an opportunity for creating a shared and personal learning process. A given reality emerged for a person (in the research project, such a reality emerged for myself and the group members) and at the same time, the person opened him/herself up to this new reality, based on his or her experience, insight and understanding.[18] Reality is

---

Journal of Narrative Therapy and Community Work, *1*. [retrieved on 13. Feb. 2018: https://narrativepractices.com.au/attach/pdf/Outsider_Witness_Common_Questions.pdf].
17 See Duncan, B. (2014). *On Becoming a Better Therapist: Evidence-Based Practice One Client at a Time*, 2nd edition, Chapter 1. Washington, DC: American Psychological Association.
18 I refer to the German education scholar Wolfgang Klafki: Klafki W (1985/1991 [expanded edition]). *Neue Studien zur Bildungstheorie und Didaktik. Zeitgemäße Allgemeinbildung und*

explored anew and emerges as meaningful to the focus person, with a value that may not have been previously appreciated or realized. Through the dialogue the individual's perception of reality is challenged, and a need for further exploration arises. Here, coaching becomes a part of the person's self-formation through a process of continuous self-development that includes virtually all situations in his personal and working life.

Viewing third-generation coaching as a dialogue form in a societal perspective

I am often asked whether it might not be time to jettison the coaching concept. I agree that the concept is somewhat tired, and that it has become burdened with associations that I would want to distance myself from. In many regards, *mentoring* in its current meaning is a fairly apt term for the dialogue form that I strive for. The mentor acts as a volunteer, unpaid adviser or trainer. It is therefore important to fashion the conversation in such a way that it is also rewarding for the mentor. Unlike the coach in a traditional coaching relationship, the mentor should benefit from his or her role. It is the *match* between the mentor and mentee that determines the success of the mentor relationship and the fruitful development of the dialogue. The main difference between mentoring and coaching is the volunteer aspect and, to some extent, the absence of professionalism. The mentee cannot expect or demand that the mentor have any professional dialogue skills. The mentor's qualifications are his or her commitment and, to some extent, seniority. Although mentoring in its current form has some of the same characteristics as third-generation coaching, the mentor often lacks the professional qualifications that professional dialogue partners should be required to attain through quality training.

Defining third-generation coaching

My own earliest definition of coaching stems from my first published book, *Coaching – Læring og Udvikling* (*Coaching – Learning and Development*) from 2002. I still embrace this definition, with a minor update:

> Coaching is participation in the dialogue partner's/group's development and learning process.[19]

---

kritisch-konstruktive Didaktik. Weinheim: Beltz Verlag; Klafki W (2000) Didaktik analysis as the core of preparation of instruction. In: Westbury, I., Hopmann, S. & Riquarts, K. (eds.). *Teaching as a Reflective Practice: The German Didaktik Tradition*. Mahwah: Lawrence Erlbaum Associates, pp. 197–206.

19 As the attentive reader will have noticed, I used the term 'focus person' in my first book, *Coaching*, and the term 'coachee' in the book *Third-Generation Coaching*. In the present context, I use the term 'dialogue partner' because I wish to include both coaching and, more broadly, professional everyday dialogues.

The key word in this definition is *participation*, which references a larger theory on learning and development: the situated learning theory developed by Lave and Wenger.[20] The theory of situated learning shifts attention away from learning in school contexts (such as formalized learning in school) and thus offers a critical alternative to functionalist understandings of knowledge and learning. Situated learning and development take place in practice communities, for example through fruitful dialogues, constituting a new form of collective learning where the participants have access to a practice ground in certain situations and thus a chance to develop in a learning community with others. Another concept is *legitimate peripheral participation*, where no single person takes centre stage. Anyone who is a recognized member of a practice community is legitimate – everyone should feel included as a member. All the parties in the practice community are more or less peripheral, depending on the situation they find themselves in and on their qualifications, understanding and interest in relation to the given task, topic and so forth. In the fruitful and transformative dialogue and learning practice, the dialogue guide (coach, teacher, manager, experienced practitioner) acts as the leader and co-reflecting interlocutor. The dialogue guide should not appear as an external expert but enters into a learning community where knowledge is viewed as a discursive phenomenon, and where everybody contributes to the shared meaning-making and the generation of knowledge. There is no final answer; knowledge is contextual and situated.

I also have a more complex definition of third-generation coaching, which includes the theoretical foundation of my understanding of dialogues, which are

- the phenomenological existentialist position;
- the narrative co-creative position.

Both positions are, however, closely interrelated in the actual dialogue practice and should only be treated as distinct and separate for analytical purposes. This expanded definition further clarifies that third-generation coaching is moving towards a reciprocal relationship where the dialogue may be reward for both (or all of the) parties. This definition goes as follows:

> Coaching is described as a developing conversation and dialogue, a co-creative process between coach and coachee with the purpose of giving (especially) the coachee room and opportunity to linger on, reflect on and gain a new understanding of his or her 1) own experiences in the specific context and 2) interactions, relationships and negotiations with others in specific contexts and situations. This coaching conversation should enable new possibilities of action within the contexts that the conversation addresses.

---

20 Lave, J. & Wenger, E. (1991). *Situated Learning. Legitimate Peripheral Participation*. Cambridge, UK: Cambridge University Press, and: Wenger, E. (1998). *Communities of Practice. Learning, Meaning, and Identity*. Cambridge, UK: Cambridge University Press.

The key purposes of third-generation coaching and fruitful dialogues

Based on the latter definition, three key purposes emerge, which are closely interrelated in the dialogue process:

1. The dialogue invites self-reflection, mainly by virtue of what Ole Fogh Kirkeby calls 'the principle of translocutionarity':[21] I do not know what I mean until I hear what I am saying; I am made to listen to myself by speaking to someone else. When one listens, the self occurs, that is: I meet myself in my own words. Karl Weick[22] describes this phenomenon in similar terms by linking the emerging meaning with an act: How can I know what I'm thinking before I hear what I'm saying?

    Moreover, self-reflection can be promoted by the coach's co-reflecting questions and through the witnessing by the coach and other dialogue participants. The coach or the group members act as co-reflecting partners, offering feedback to the focus person's statements. We develop self-reflection by being involved in other peoples' life perspectives. As part of the reflection process it can be helpful to acknowledge and appreciate differences or multiversity, that is, the existence of multiple local truths, which the participants present from the perspective of their own respective experiences and worldviews. We may expand and enrich our own positions by developing our ability to embrace different perceptions of reality and incorporating others' perspectives on specific challenges.
2. The dialogue aims for a *shared reflection* by the involved parties. That is the first step towards learning in practice communities. The dialogue partners create something together, new understanding and knowledge that emerges based on shared reflection, which goes beyond what a single individual can achieve.
3. The dialogue invites a shift in *perspective*. The most important purpose of coaching and fruitful dialogues is essentially to enable a shift in position and perspective and to find a new and more appropriate position. The coach's questions are intended to induce a shift in the dialogue partner's perceptions and provide impulses for a narrative shift. Ideally, the coach's questions should encourage both reflection and transformation.

Closing remarks

Certain questions have been raised about the term 'coaching', but I choose to continue to use it – in part for want of a better alternative. My ambition is not to

---

21 Kirkeby, O. F. (2009). *The New Protreptic – The Concept and the Art.* Copenhagen: Copenhagen Business School Press. (Distributed by Marston Book Service).
22 Weick, K. E. (1979). *The Social Psychology of Organizing* (2nd edition). New York: McGraw Hill (p. 133).

replace the term with something else, but instead to develop the coaching profession, clarifying its role in relation to the current requirements of coaching. I view third-generation coaching as a necessary development and define the approach as an open, fruitful and transformative dialogue that, ideally, unfolds in a reciprocal relationship between both or all of the dialogue partners. Coaching should move away from a narrow focus on goals and performance and instead contribute to the art of lingering in dialogue. Through self-reflection and shared reflections between the dialogue guide and the dialogue partner, this dialogue should result in a new position that is enriching for one's life in general or in relation to the specific situations or topics that were the focus of the conversation.

Chaper 2

The societal context
The emergence of the achievement-subject and the burnout society

In this chapter I take a critical look at developments in society that ultimately have consequences for coaching conversations and other everyday professional dialogues and the way they should be conducted. In the past, one could point to a clearly identifiable external enemy. In today's globalized world, that is much harder to do, and in order to handle the many stressful situations in their work and personal life, individuals instead begin to direct criticism at themselves. Driven by feelings of personal inadequacy, they attempt to act in order to avoid losing their grip and turn to coaching, mindfulness, fitness and other development 'tools' and activities in order to survive. This may prove counterproductive, however, and risks further exacerbating the personal erosion they are experiencing. Loneliness, fatigue, burnout, stress, depression and ADHD are increasingly common psychological mass phenomena in today's society and workplace accomplishments are seen as the ultimate yardstick for development and success. The hyperactivity and multitasking of everyday life degrades us to an animal laborans – a working animal. On this background, I state my wish and formulate the following thesis: we need to revitalize and relearn the art of lingering in the moment. Third-generation coaching and fruitful dialogues are some of the means that can help us achieve the necessary reorientation and rootedness.

Neoliberalism and New Public Management promote self-criticism and self-control

Today's Western societies are influenced by neoliberal thinking and New Public Management strategies, a trend that many social and political scientists regard as dysfunctional.[1] The core idea driving this development is the pursuit of economic efficiency based on market-based management and regulation mechanisms, which puts democratic principles and other forms of legitimacy under severe pressure. Ultimately, this neoliberal doctrine leads to growing economic and social imbalances, where the rich get richer, and economic and social inequality becomes

---

1 Harvey, D. (2005). *A Brief History of Neoliberalism*. Oxford: Oxford University Press.

more pronounced. Competition among institutions (for example hospitals, schools or service providers), increased data-driven supervisory systems in public institutions, ranking systems and a constant focus on optimizing efficiency permeate all aspects of society, including both private and public organizations. The growing pressures on individual sectors and organizations (such as the healthcare sector and individual hospitals) impact individual employees, who are in direct competition with their co-workers and thus need to be better and more efficient in order to have a secure foothold on the job market. This individualization is manifest, in part, in individual pay agreements, bonus schemes, allowances, flexible hours and functions and a growing responsibility for one's own work schedule and tasks – known in modern management speak as 'self-management' – a form of self-management that ultimately results in *self-criticism*. In recent years, the Danish sociologist Rasmus Willig has warned against this trend; in a newspaper interview he frames the issue in the following terms:

> That is a profound shift, because as soon as the criticism becomes an internal issue, it leads to a new kind of silence, as no one wants to put their own problems on display. That would amount to labelling oneself a loser, someone who is incapable of meeting the increasing demand to embrace change and be prepared to compete on market terms.[2]

In the interview Willig highlights the intense individualization of the challenges we all face. We are generally afraid to be open to others, afraid to display signs of weakness. In a culture where we chase 'likes' and carefully engineer positive presentations of ourselves and our lives, insecurity and self-doubt have no place in the face we present to the outside world. Far too often, we keep problems and difficulties to ourselves. A new dialogue culture, framed by solidarity, could help take some of the pressure off the individual.

The freedom paradox

The disciplinary society that existed for the past two centuries, and which Foucault wrote about in his classic texts,[3] no longer exists. Then, disciplining was framed by relatively transparent hierarchical structures and clear legal and political instruments of power. The power of the state-shaped human relations. In the disciplinary age, people were told what to do, and they were soon put on notice if their performance was unsatisfactory, often in the form of explicit reprimands or punishment. But at least, people knew what was expected of them, and what they needed to do to be approved. The disciplinary society has now been replaced

---

2 www.b.dk/kultur/nu-er-det-din-egen-skyld-hvis-livet-gaar-skaevt# [download 1.11.15]; see also his book: Willig, R. (2013). *Kritikkens U-vending*. Copenhagen: Hans Reitzels Forlag.
3 E.g., Foucault, M. (1991). *Discipline and Punish, the Birth of the Prison*. London: Penguin Books.

by an *achievement society* with self-management, self-monitoring and self-control as the key mechanisms of control. And these mechanisms are *individual*. Self-criticism and self-doubt thus become the individual's constant companions. The disciplinary power that once rested with the authorities or authority figures now resides in the individuals themselves. Formally speaking, we all have a wide range of liberties and are free to do what we want, but we have become our own, ever-vigilant individual supervisors – our own worst enemies. Byung-Chul Han, a social critic who speaks within a philosophical framework, has described the freedom paradox as follows:

> The achievement-subject stands free from any external instance of domination [Herrschaftsinstanz] forcing it into work, much less exploiting it. It is lord and master of itself. It is subject to no one – or, as the case may be, only to itself. It differs from the obedience-subject on this score. However, the disappearance of domination does not entail freedom. Instead, it makes freedom and constraint coincide.[4]

Today's freedom paradox thus contributes crucially to the self-exploitation that is in fact much more effective than the exploitation by others that characterized the disciplinary society. In principle, we have the freedom not to, but we choose – or are drawn, perhaps – to exploit ourselves. Han makes an additional point, which is crucial for the psychological consequences of this freedom paradox on the individual: 'The psychic indispositions of achievement are pathological manifestations of such a paradoxical freedom'.[5]

Han's analysis is rarely explicitly present in our individual awareness – if it were, we would probably be in a much better place! The freedom paradox sneaks up on us, as individuals, gradually shaping our mental well-being. When it becomes too much, we begin to feel fatigued, exhausted, irritable; if we fail to heed the warning signals we ultimately end up with burnout and stress.

Burnout society

Based on the growing prevalence of psychological dysfunction, such as attention deficit, exhaustion, depression and stress, Han introduced the concept of the *burnout society*. His description of the historical development over the past 100 years can be summarized as follows: during the twentieth century we lived in an *immunological age* with clear distinctions between internal and external, friend

---

4   Han, B. (2015). *The Burnout Society*. Redwood City, CA: Stanford University Press, p. 11. Han, originally from South Korea, is considered the new 'hot shot' in German philosophy and social criticism. He is just about to be better known in the English-speaking world as several of his books have recently been translated books into English. Han has been an important source of inspiration for me, also for the present book.
5   Ibid., p. 11.

and foe, own and alien. Virus was the metaphor of the age. The Cold War was a phenomenon of the time. It was possible to identify an external enemy. The immune system has to be able to fight off the virus.

Han argues that the previous immunological paradigm is incompatible with the globalization process. The dialectics of negativity, the principal characteristic of immunity, still perseveres in certain groups (for example due to fear of the unknown or the unfamiliar) and may become manifest as racism.[6] What is foreign is only acceptable as something exotic, as a travel destination. However, as a consequence of the many changes and globalization processes we are clearly moving in a different direction. Han describes this development as an *excess of positivity*, due to overproduction, overcapacity and overcommunication. He adds, 'Rejection occurring in response to excess positivity does not amount to immunological defense, but to digestive-neuronal abreaction'.[7] This form of reaction characterizes the psychological dysfunctions in the burnout society, which we as individuals and *achievement-subjects* succumb to when we fail to live up to our own ambitions and demands, or when we are overwhelmed by overinformation and overcommunication, paralyzed and at risk of burnout, stress and depression.[8]

The dissolution of time and space

Fatigue and burnout also stem from our current perception of time and the way in which we structure time and space in our subjective perceptual world. Here, the digitization affects us in new ways, where we can barely grasp the consequences, whether for the individual or for humanity at large. In a pre-industrial world, where people lived in tune with nature, time was perceived as cyclical. Life was governed by the seasonal cycles, and time was structured in step with natural variations and diurnal rhythms. The onset of industrialization altered the structure of time. Time was now perceived as linear. The pace of the working day was no longer determined by natural conditions. Now, the factory picked arbitrary times that marked the beginning and the end of the working day. The clock became an important instrument, which reflected the linear view of time. It was important to keep track of time. Human working procedures were synchronized with the clock, and especially after the introduction of shift work, the diurnal rhythm became secondary. Time and space, however, were still perceived as related.

---

6 See Han's article in the Danish newspaper *Information*, 10 February 2015: www.information.dk/523950 [retrieved 1 November 2015]. Here, Han also writes, 'The Pegida movement would have a hard time gaining ground in Hamburg, since here, distress and anxiety are individualized'.
7 Han (2015). Burnout society, p. 5.
8 A key publication is this one, by the French sociologist Alain Ehrenberg (2009). *The Weariness of the Self: Diagnosing the History of Depression in the Contemporary Age*. Montreal: McGill-Queen's University Press.

With the advance of digitization and globalization, the linear structure disappears, and time loses its spatial framework. Digital communication dissolves the sense of a unity of time and space. The Internet and email know no physical boundaries. Messages are no longer conveyed in tangible form from one place to another. No one waits for the mailman anymore; the messages simply pop up on the screen in a steady flow. The time that passes from when someone sends a message until it reaches the recipient approaches zero. Electronic mail is detached from time and space, with everything that this implies. Social communities are increasingly formed in virtual settings, and the number of 'friends' often exceeds one's mental capacity to relate. Communication is often reduced to self-presentation in social media, and people live and breathe by 'likes' and thumbs-up. The information flow requires increasing multitasking, which favours superficial attention and a lack of focused presence in the moment. When this state takes over, it can lead to a meltdown, where everything seems overwhelming, and where the messages lead to disorientation and cease to be meaningful to the individual recipient.

Concurrent sense of acceleration and stagnation

The dissolution of time and space and the acceleration and vast amount of information we are constantly subjected to are among the main causes of the massive growth in the aforementioned *digestive-neuronal abreaction*, which describes the mental meltdown of the fatigue society. We are unable to digest the flow of information at the rate we receive it. The many messages and inputs make it impossible for us to maintain a *narrative orbit*, as Byung-Chul Han puts it.[9] The information flow results in mental flooding or constipation, and at worst, we experience 'everything' to be meaningless.

In Han's view, this acceleration has a companion, which Han does not perceive as a negative factor but rather as a consequence of the acceleration processes. He speaks of the *deceleration* that emerges when we feel rudderless, disoriented and no longer know where we are going. Acceleration and deceleration are two sides of the same coin. Both have roots in the increasing narrative tempo.[10] We can no longer form a meaningful connection between certain events and string them together to form a timeline that lets us shape a narrative with a coherent plot. The plot is what lends the story meaning and coherence. However, when we increasingly struggle with differentiating between meaningful and meaningless, we lose this inner sense of coherence that feeds the narrative. In order to form a

---

9 Han, B.-C. (2017). *The Scent of Time: A Philosophical Essay on the Art of Lingering*. Cambridge, UK: Polity Press. On p. 23, Han writes, 'If this narrative orbit of history decays, there is also a massification of events and information'. The title of Han's book was a key source of inspiration that helped shape the direction of this book.
10 Ibid., the link between acceleration and deceleration is described on pp. 23–24. On p. 25, Han speaks of 'an increasing narrative tempo'.

narrative, *my* narrative, I have to be able to differentiate and sort. We need an 'inner compass' in order to imbue events and actors with meaning, and the narrative structure, in turn, helps shape our inner compass.

Han says that we are living in an *age of whizzing*, which has replaced the previous century's *age of marching*.[11] Previously, we knew what direction to take. It was more or less decided from above – by official authorities. Marching was determined by a certain rhythm, direction and group cohesion. Now, we are like flies on a glass wall, whizzing about – disoriented, without ever getting anywhere and, ultimately, despairing. *Whizzing* becomes the metaphor for a diffuse and hectic life, and whizzing becomes synonymous with the fusion of acceleration and stagnation. Individuals move at a feverish pace without ever going anywhere – eventually succumbing to complete exhaustion.

Reinstating lingering

Many of the 'development tools' that are on offer (such as coaching, mindfulness and fitness) are intended as kindly help to the tired, exhausted, stressed people living in today's society, who spend too much time whizzing and are no longer able to settle and find their way in life. Sadly, these development tools may perpetuate and exacerbate the state of whizzing, unless they are applied with care; they risk pushing the subject further down a path where he or she expects to find infinite possibilities for development of their own potential. The current emphasis on positive thinking tells us this is possible, but an individual who is on the verge of a breakdown needs a different reality. The achievement-subject, who has reached his or her limits, must be met with nurturing and understanding. Tools that only help the person squeeze out the last few drops have the opposite effect in the long run. It is time to challenge the existing discourse that characterizes the achievement society, with the individual's strong urge to exercise self-control and self-monitoring.

We need to pause, come face to face with ourselves and each other in a focused presence that differs from the often superficial communication that takes place via email and social media. I am definitely no Luddite, suggesting that everyone has to shut down their Facebook profile. However, we should take the warning signs seriously. The number of people succumbing to stress has been steadily rising over the past decades. Currently, 25 per cent of women and 17.5 per cent of men in Denmark are experiencing unhealthy stress levels. For women under 24 years of age, the share is 33 per cent, which must be considered very dramatic.[12] The World Health Organization warns that stress has become a 'World Wide Epidemic'. Something has to change!

---

11 Ibid.
12 Sundhedsstyrelsen. *Danskernes sundhed. Det nationale sundhedsprofil 2013.* http://sundhedsstyrelsen. dk/~/media/1529A4BCF9C64905BAC650B6C45B72A5.ashx [download 20 Feb. 2018].

Closing remarks

Through a brief analysis of social changes over the past two decades I have sought to set the stage for challenging coaching as a 'development tool' that is exclusively intended to help people handle ever growing workloads. I thus support the criticism that has been raised by social critics and scholars, who warn against the consequences of this growing emphasis on self-control and urge for development. It is my hope and my ambition to invite you, the reader, to rethink coaching and other so-called development dialogues by laying a new foundation for conversations that offer time and space for reflection and contemplation, where we learn to linger in order to get to know and understand each other and ourselves better.

Chapter 3

Searching for one's own self
Identity as one of the key challenges of our time

Identity formation and the development of the self are key challenges in a time when the scope and complexity of our social relationships are expanding to an extreme degree, especially through the many contacts and interactions we engage in via digital media and the flood of information that washes over us every day. The rapid pace of information sharing is eroding our individual sense of time and space as stabilizing factors. Our body awareness and its ability to act as a sensory anchor for our identity formation are being undermined by the virtual spaces where we spend more and more time.

In this chapter I address the fundamental interaction at play in identity formation between being oneself and being shaped by others. I address a wide range of theoretical positions and reflections to present a variety of understandings of identity and self-concept. However, it is difficult for us as individuals to escape from an often invisible power discourse that compels us to keep ourselves in check and makes freedom seem overwhelming and impossible to handle. This places individuals under enormous pressure. We self-monitor in a way that risks leading to self-doubt, burnout, stress and other psychological dysfunctions. Can coaching and other fruitful dialogues play a role by offering a space for self-reflection and identity development and, perhaps, by providing a sort of anchor or counterbalance to the prevailing discourse?

Identity research is highly topical

Over the years I have repeatedly dealt with the issues of identity and self-concept from many different angles. In a dissertation I wrote in the early 1990s I emphasized the role of social settings and contexts for identity formation.[1] I have also explored links between body and identity[2] that appears particularly topical

---

1   Stelter, R. (1996). *Du bist wie dein Sport – Studien zur Entwicklung von Selbstkonzept und Identität*. Schorndorf: Hofmann Verlag. Article on this topic: Stelter, R. (1998). The body, self and identity. Personal and social constructions of the self through sport and movement (review article). *European Yearbook of Sport Psychology*, 2, 1–32.
2   See, especially, my three chapters in: Schilhab, T. S. S., Juelskjær, M. & Moser, T. (eds.) (2008). *The Learning Body*. Copenhagen: DPU Forlag.

today, as individuals are losing their bodies in the virtual realm. In relation to coaching and other spaces of learning and development, the connection between identity and self-concept is particularly relevant. Ever since my earlier books on coaching this aspect has thus played a prominent role.

Identity is a major research topic[3] across the research literature, spanning from sociology, psychology and philosophy to political science, cultural studies and teaching.[4] The distinction between the concepts of identity and self has been widely discussed in literature. The distinction between identity and self can be clarified with the following definitions: *identity* pertains to the dynamic process and interaction between the individual and the social environment, while the *self* is the concept best suited to operationalize and capture certain characteristics in an individual, such as thoughts and feelings related to the self. This is reflected in countless terms prefixed by 'self': self-concept, self-esteem, self-destruction, self-development and so forth. The two American psychologists Markus and Wurf define self-concept as

> a dynamic interpretive structure that mediates most significant intrapersonal processes (including information processing, affect, and motivation) and a wide variety of interpersonal processes (including social perception; choice of situation, partner, and interaction strategy; and reaction to feedback).[5]

Self-concept is the driver of identity formation, and in many ways it is the basis of coaching and developmental dialogues, where the individual wants to examine him/herself, often with a desire to find a slightly different way of being. Successful identity formation basically revolves around striking a balance between being unique while achieving a sense of attachment and similarity with others, also in relation to one's biographical course of development.[6]

The emergence of identity theories

For millennia, humanity has wondered and examined *who we are, how to live* and *how our personalities are formed* and thus, in the widest sense, addressing identity and self: Confucius, Plato, Aristotle, Epicurus, Augustine, Marcus Aurelius, Hildegard of Bingen, Meister Eckhart, Immanuel Kant, Søren Kierkegaard, Wilhelm James, George Herbert Mead, Eric Erikson, Erving Goffman and Kenneth

---

3 A search for 'identitet' [Danish for 'identity'] in REX, the electronic database of the Royal Danish Library yields man 858,960 references (4 November 2015). There is even a magazine dedicated to the topic: *Identity: An International Journal of Theory and Research*.
4 A good introduction is Schwartz, S. J., Luyckx, K. & Vignoles, V. L. (eds.) (2011). *Handbook of Identity Theory and Research*. New York, NY: Springer.
5 Markus, H. & Wurf, E. (1987). The dynamic self-concept. A psychological perspective. *Annual Review of Psychology*, 38, s. 300.
6 See more in Bamberg, M., De Fina, A. & Schiffrin, D. (2011). Discourse and identity construction. In S. J. Schwartz *et al.* (eds.), *Handbook of Identity Theory and Research*. Dordrecht: Springer.

Gergen constitute a more or less representative selection of thinkers who have been key in this field. In the past, these topics were the domain of philosophers and theologians. However, it is only with the systematic development of psychology and sociology as scientific fields in the late nineteenth century that it becomes possible to speak of identity theories in a modern sense – not to diminish the important contributions of the classical philosophers. More on this topic later. Identity studies only became necessary with the advent of modernity, as the individual was now required to *take responsibility* for his or her own life. Previously, people viewed their fate as predetermined by God.

Immanuel Kant, the important German philosopher of the Enlightenment, introduced the transcendental understanding that I wish to highlight here, because it fundamentally shapes our understanding of the self, and because it impacts later philosophical and psychological understandings of self-awareness. According to Kant,[7] the self is given as a transcendental condition – a *transcendental ego*. Thus, the individual does not have direct access to him/herself. Only in hindsight and in an underlying stream of consciousness can an individual ever understand him/herself. According to Kant, the self is the condition and the prerequisite of (self-)perception, and it cannot therefore simultaneously be an object of the perception process. The important phenomenologist Edmund Husserl later returned to the concept of the transcendental self, but he believed that it was possible to approach one's self via *epoché*,[8] which includes bracketing self-judgement in order to approach the self.

William James[9] laid a foundation for modern identity studies with the chapter 'The conscious of self' in his classic two-volume publication from 1890 *The Principles of Psychology*. Like Kant he argued that the individual does not have direct access to his or her own subjectivity. He distinguishes between *empirical self*, which he calls 'me' and *the pure ego*, which he calls 'I'. The object of self-reflection is the *empirical self*, which forms the basis of what we call self-concept. *The pure ego*, in James' analysis, contains the human consciousness of our own immediate and absolute (transcendental) subjectivity, which we can never truly come into contact with.[10] By introducing the concept of an *empirical self* James

---

7 Kant, I. (1901). *Immanuel Kant's Kritik der reinen Vernunft, Sämmtliche Werke*, 1. Band (8. revidierte Auflage ed., Philosophische Bibliothek Band 37). (Original from 1781). English from 2003: Critique of Pure Reason (Dover Philosophical Classics). Mineola, NY: Dover Publications.
8 Discussed in more detail in Husserl, E. (1995). *Ideen zu einer Reinen Phänomenologie und Phänomenologischen Philosophie* (vol. 1). Heidelberg: Springer (original from 1913). English translation from 1982: *Ideas Pertaining to a Pure Phenomenology and to a Phenomenological Philosophy – First Book: General Introduction to a Pure Phenomenology* (Kersten, F., trans.). The Hague: Nijhoff.
9 James, W. (1890). *The Principles of Psychology*. New York: Holt.
10 James builds on Kant's transcendental philosophy. James is a leading representative of pragmatism, a school of philosophy that emerged in the United States, which anchors perception in concrete action. James's concept of *the pure ego* can be related to Kant's transcendental ego. See also Pihlström, S. (2010). Kant and pragmatism. *Pragmatism Today*, 1, 2, 50–61.

makes it possible for dialogue guides and partners to deal with the self via self-reflection. We can make the self the object of our reflection, either on our own or with someone else/others in dialogue. As individuals, we may also come to understand ourselves better, in hindsight, by examining our actions and behaviour in interactions with relevant others.

Just under 50 years later Mead[11] concluded that our individual self-concept is not only developed via interactions with specific others in a face-to-face dialogue, but via more general influences mediated by the norms, values, attitudes and perceptions of our social environment. He called this *the generalized other* and saw it as determining our way of being in the world. In an understanding that is not far removed from James's notion of *the pure ego* Mead describes a person's spontaneous reactions in certain situations and the immediate and original aspects of these reactions as 'I' – also with inspiration from Kant's thinking. As individuals we are influenced and shaped by our experiences and interpretations of our social environment. Mead calls this part of the self 'me'. He sees it as unfolding via *the generalized other* and describes it as the part of the personality that we, as individuals, have access to via acting, reflecting and thinking.

The theorists Mead and James both draw on Kant's thinking in their basic ideas, and they introduce a basic epistemological position that may be crucial for our understanding of the self. The transcendental philosophical position postulates a self that exists 'a priori' – for example, *the pure ego* – which we cannot access via our own experience, but which is presumed to exist. 'Ego', the person as such – the 'Ding an sich' (Kant) – is not accessible to our perception, neither to an outside person nor to an outside observer. The epistemological position, which assumes that there is something that I, as an individual, do not have access to, is a core aspect of many identity theories. It is this 'Ego' or 'I' that I attempt to approach via coaching and other forms of dialogues; that is, through another, who asks questions about me and reflects along with me. Particularly in first-generation coaching, with its goal-driven purpose, the focus will be on the individual and on examining and revealing his or her inherent potential in order to help the person achieve a goal. Coaching with a more philosophical and in-depth approach will instead examine how the individual's fundamental assumptions, values and morals shape his or her actions.

The systemic-social-constructionist tradition, by contrast, focuses on the *relationship*. Here, it is assumed that the individual is purely a product of his or her relations with others. The transcendental (*the pure ego*) is not addressed – even as a fictive assumption. In a comment on Martin Buber's book *I and Thou*, which underscores the dialogue partner's impact on one's self-concept, the leading social-constructionist psychologist Kenneth Gergen says, 'Yet, while these works have been inspiring, they still retain what for me are problematic

---

11 Mead, G. H. (2015). *Mind, Self and Society*. Original from 1934. Chicago: University of Chicago Press.

vestiges of the individualist tradition'.[12] He describes his own relational position as follows:[13]

> Relationships move on, carrying with them the identities of the participants. An infinite unfolding over which no *one* has control. Like an ocean wave, the "I" may appear for a frozen moment to be itself alone. Yet, as the moment passes the wave disappears into the endless undulations from which it is inseparable.

In my own work I draw on an amalgam of traditions – or, one might say, I avoid opting for one over another by navigating between the front lines of this dispute. Still, I am guided by the following clear assumption:[14] As humans, we have a definite drive, intentionality or direction that causes us, as individuals, to always take a proactive stance to our environments and ourselves. The self exists before our experience (a priori), but it is also the key premise of our experiences, as individuals. Moreover, I assume that an individual is shaped in interactions with others, framed by the relationships, contexts and culture(s) he or she is a part of. The amalgamation of these theoretical positions also plays an important role in my discussion of third-generation coaching and co-creative dialogues later in this book.

Identity and self-reflexivity in late modern society

The British sociologist Anthony Giddens has examined how individuals are affected by the profound social change processes that take place in the late modern age. In connection with this work he introduces the concept of reflexivity, which he describes as the continuous revision on the basis of new information that is characteristic and necessary in late modern society. Giddens writes:[15]

> Each of us not only "has", but lives a biography reflexively organised in terms of flows of social and psychological information about possible ways of life. Modernity is a post-traditional order, in which the question, "How shall I live?" has to be answered in day-to-day decisions about how to behave, what to wear and what to eat – and many other things – as well as interpreted within the temporal unfolding of self-identity.

---

12 Gergen, K. J. (2009). *Relational Being. Beyond Self and Community.* Oxford: Oxford University Press, p. 21.
13 Ibid., pp. 45–46.
14 This assumption is of a character that no scholar or thinker can ultimately reject or verify it. Thus, assumptions have heuristic function. They need to prove their worth in practice.
15 Giddens, A. (1997). *Modernity and Self-Identity. Self and Society in the Late Modern Age.* Stanford, CA: Stanford University Press, p. 14.

Theoretical basis

Giddens considers the development of self-identity as the individual's constantly unfolding reflexive project. He describes self-reflexivity as 'the process whereby self-identity is constituted by the reflexive structuring of self-narratives'.[16] He also speaks of 'institutional reflexivity', on the other hand: 'the reflexivity of modernity, involving the routine incorporation of new knowledge or information into environments of action that are thereby reconstituted or reorganised'.[17] Giddens describes reflexivity as follows:[18]

> The reflexivity of modernity extends into the core of the self. Put in another way, in a post-traditional order becomes a reflexive project. . . . Modernity, it might be said, breaks down the protective framework of the small community, and of tradition, replacing these with much larger, impersonal organisations. The individual feels bereft and alone in a world in which he or she lacks the psychological support and the sense of security provided by more traditional settings.

By describing *the self as a reflexive project* Giddens points to the key identity-related challenge and thus proposes a motivation for the advent of coaching by mentioning the need for a reflective space in late modern society. However, his understanding of self-reflection has little to do with an approach to coaching that strives only to clarify goals and finding a quick fix – the approach that I describe as first-generation coaching. Thus, although Giddens does not mention coaching, he can be understood as an advocate of a dialogue form that is in-depth and reflective, and thus constitutes a form of third-generation coaching.

The social construction of the self

The self-reflecting subject has become a prominent phenomenon in our time and has taken on great importance in the permanent identity effort that each of us engages in. Here, coaching, therapeutic conversations or 'simply' a good talk with a friend has a crucial function by offering a space for self-reflection and shared reflection.

Today, we all enter into countless social relationships, both in 'real life' and in the virtual world. On social media in particular, many have scores of *friends*, and people are interconnected in multiple complex networks. Digital algorithms compel the users to address and consider constantly how to deal with new emerging options for expanding their network even more. Meanwhile, the individual users receive 'likes', invitations, comments and assessment, particularly on Facebook and other social and professional digital networks (such as LinkedIn,

---

16 Ibid., p. 244.
17 Ibid., p. 243.
18 Ibid., pp. 32–34.

ResearchGate and so forth).[19] Social media promote individuals' urge for self-monitoring and exercise a power of the person that he or she has willingly submitted to. At times, participation in the network can lead to feelings of inadequacy and stress. Our involvement in these countless relationships has a definite impact on our self-concept and identity and may ultimately jeopardize our personal freedom.[20]

Our selves are constantly shaped and expanded. At the same time, we find it increasingly difficult to hold on to anything even resembling stability. We struggle to liberate ourselves from outside assessments, which shape our self-concept. All our relations – real as well as virtual – leave an imprint on us as individuals, which affect the way we perceive ourselves and the way we act in certain social contexts and virtual forums. Our individual self-concept and identity depend, to a high degree, on the relationships, contexts and cultures that we are involved in. And in this process the self becomes relational, as described extensively by Gergen.[21]

This theoretical angle, which emphasizes relational interpersonal dynamics, appears to constitute a necessary step in a new direction, considering the impact of societal changes on our self-formation and identity formation. To develop a theory that is capable of capturing the growing diversification of individual lifestyles and the individual's attachment to many different social contexts, we should abandon an exclusively egocentric, individualist notion of identity and instead embrace and incorporate theories that rest on sociocentric assumptions. The sociocentric, relational and social-constructionist direction aims to examine the self within a system of diverse social relationships and varying social settings. The need to seek new explanations of the interaction between the individual and the individual's complex environment is driven by changes in the social environment. That has led to the development of social-constructionist theory, with Gergen as a key representative. In this framework the self is regarded as a social construct[22] – created through the relationships the subject engages in, and continuously rooted in varying social contexts. This perspective clearly moves away from a position that regards the individual as an autonomous and self-determined entity. The theoretical perspective changes completely: perception, cognition and emotions are anchored in the relationships as 'the property of ongoing relationships', as Gergen[23] puts it, no longer the personal property of any one individual, as assumed in traditional psychological theories.

---

19 An overview of how the digital world affects the human self can be found, for example, in an article by Russell W. Belk (2013). 'Extended self in a digital world'. *Journal of Consumer Research*, vol. 40, pp. 477–500.
20 The German-Korean philosopher Byung-Chul Han has addressed this issue in his book from 2017 *Psychopolitics – Neoliberalism and New Technologies of Power*. London & Brooklyn NY: Verso.
21 For example in Gergen, K. J. (2009). *Relational Being*. Oxford: Oxford University Press.
22 Gergen ibid. and Gergen, K. J. (2008). *An Invitation to Social Construction*. (2nd edition). London: Sage.
23 Gergen, 2008, p. 106.

Identity is shaped in one way in one setting (for example, in the workplace), in another way in another setting (for example, in the family) and in a third way on Facebook; we negotiate our identity or present ourselves differently, depending on the given social setting. In the late modern and postmodern age, personal identity becomes an increasingly complex process. Some speak of a patchwork identity,[24] as we shape and construct ourselves differently in different contexts. In a sense, an individual may be several persons within one, and we may have very different perceptions of ourselves depending on the given situation and social setting. The individual, context-dependent, 'patches' in this 'quilt' describe the diversity of possible behaviours and self-presentations that each of us has access to. However, when we examine a person's patchwork identity as a whole, we hopefully discern a coherent image nonetheless. The person will also be able to achieve some form of stability in his or her self-presentation by seeking out the same social settings over and over again in order to achieve self-affirming feedback,[25] that is, feedback that confirms their own self-image.

The performative self

In order to handle the identity challenges of today's society, the individual has to engage actively in a sort of *negotiation* about his or her own identity. As with any task, some people master this task better than others, by virtue of their mental capacity, education or social position. For example, it is crucial to be able to build a social network, where one can negotiate a fairly consistent identity. Further, it is clearly helpful to possess rhetorical skills that make it easier to justify and argue for one's choices, preferences and thus, ultimately, one's identity position. As a fairly new development, one also has to be able to develop a certain degree of resilience in face of the constant assessment that is particularly pronounced in digital media. Here lies a danger that few can fathom, let alone handle.

In the traditional order that Giddens mentioned, the protective framework of the small community, identity was more or less something that was issued at birth. People were embedded in stable social relations and a stable social structure that left little opportunity for moving beyond one's original social class. Nowadays, identity is hard work, and self-presentation, self-fashioning and self-stabilization[26] are key aspects of everyday life.

In the social construction of the self, two aspects in particular must always be dynamically interconnected:

---

24 Keupp *et al.* (1999). *Identitätskonstruktionen. Das Patchwork der Identitäten in der Spätmoderne.* Reinbek: Rowohlt.
25 See Swann, W. B. Jr. (1987). Identity negotiation: Where two roads meet. *Journal of Personality and Social Psychology*, 53, 1038–1051.
26 I am convinced that we will see a growing trend of individuals trying to find more permanent points to hold on to in their identity development (cf. Brinkmann's book *Stand firm* (2017), which appears to have hit a nerve).

- Individuals need to develop a self-concept and a self-image as a result of the interactions, relationships, contexts and cultures that they are part of.
- Individuals need to develop proactive ways to create themselves and present themselves to their environment. A key concept here is self-fashioning[27] or *staging the self*,[28] that is, the person's active and more or less deliberate way of creating a scenic stage for his or her self and aspirations. This performative drive and the staging of the self can be defined as the purposeful display (or suppression) of behaviours that are relevant to the form that reflects the person's emerging social identity.[29]

This performative aspect of the self is becoming increasingly important for our ability to preserve some degree of control over our identity. This theory is not exactly new, as it has played a role in modern social sciences for many years, but it has gained greater importance today, because the number of 'stages' an individual performs on or creates is growing steadily.

The American sociologist and social psychologist Erving Goffman is a prominent theorist who published his now-classic *The Presentation of Self in Everyday Life*[30] in 1959. Goffman underscored the need for individuals to secure and present their identities in dialogue with their social environments. The person, so to speak, performs a character on stage. In Goffman's understanding, the self is *the performed character*, and he thus directs his focus squarely on the social origins of the self as a product of the interaction with our social environment. In the conclusion to his seminal book Goffman writes:[31]

> In this report the performed self was seen as some kind of image, usually creditable, which the individual on stage and in character effectively attempt to induce others to hold of him. While this image is entertained *concerning* the individual, so that a self is imputed to him, this self itself does not derive from its possessor, but from the whole scene of his action, being generated by that attribute of local events which renders them interpretable by witnesses. A correctly staged and performed scene leads the audience to impute a self to a performed character, but this imputation – this self – is a *product* of the scene, and is not a *cause* of it.

---

27 Greenblatt, S. (1980). *Renaissance Self-fashioning, from More to Shakespeare*. Chicago: University of Chicago Press.
28 A common concept in social psychology is *impression management*, a concept that I view as being broader and less closely tied to the current societal situation.
29 Klein, O. *et al.* (2007). Social identity performance: extending the strategic side of SIDE. *Personality and Social Psychology Review*, 11, 1, 29.
30 Goffman, E. (1959). *The Presentation of Self in Everyday Life*. New York: Doubleday.
31 Goffman (1959), p. 252.

A person presenting his or her self is thus likened to an actor who is able to pick his or her own stage and props. We shape, preserve and adjust our selves in the social situations that make up our lives, and identity can thus be viewed as a co-production by the individual and the social environment.

Goffman sees the human body as an important medium in this self-presentation process. For example, we can use the body to alter an 'inappropriate' appearance that others' reactions make the person aware of in a given situation. Goffman was mainly interested in the individual's striving for inner coherence, however; the self-presentation had the key purpose of achieving approval and avoiding embarrassing situations. Today's identity challenges are focused on staging the self, as the individual pursues the specific goal of *creating him/herself* and his or her own identity. This process, by necessity, takes place in interaction with the other actors on stage.

Today, the human body is used even more explicitly as a medium of self-presentation. We work out in order to optimize our physical appearance. If that does not do the job, plastic surgery can help us shape the body to match our own or socially mediated ideals. And if the body's performance is still not satisfactory, we have access to a whole new range of aids in the form of memory- and concentration-enhancing drugs, anabolic steroids, genetic engineering and so forth. Health, the right diet and fashion can also serve as important self-presentation methods to support our effort to mould a particular self. In addition, our home design, our choice of consumer goods, our travel habits and our participation in cultural events play an increasingly important role for our self-presentation. As mentioned above, digital social media have a key impact in this process.[32]

Downsides to the postmodern urge for development and self-presentation

Kenneth Gergen describes the postmodern being as a 'restless nomad'.[33] From Gergen's perspective, the postmodern self is overwhelmed by the countless possibilities and ways of being. The many relationships and contexts, real as well as virtual, that the individual has to deal with on a daily basis can lead to a sense of oversaturation and fatigue and, ultimately, doubt and disorientation about how best to act in a given context. Nomads move on to somewhere else, where the grass is, presumably, greener, and living conditions are better. But what happens for today's *restless nomads*, when the new place does not prove to be better? A growing number of people struggle with achieving a sense of stability, control

---

32 See: Schau, H. J. & Gilly, M. C. (2003). We are what we post? Self-presentation in personal web space. *Journal of Consumer Research*, 30(3), 385–404.
33 Gergen, K. J. (1991), p. 173.

and reliable landmarks. In their search for stability, more and more people pursue extreme, but socially acceptable, habits and lifestyles, such as extreme sports (iron man, 100-kilometre runs and so forth). Others succumb to the pressure, showing various forms of psychological and psychiatric dysfunction – from burnout, stress and depression to eating disorders and self-injury, such as cutting – often a cry for help and a sign that the person is losing hold of his or her sense of self. When the self-image is shattered, and the patchwork quilt begins to pull apart, the person loses his or her bearings and the fundamental sense of direction that is a prerequisite of a good life.

Identity formation and, in particular, the constant demands for performance, self-presentation and development puts the individual in a situation that never lets up; we are always 'moving on', performing and striving to live up to our own and others' expectations. If we are not moving forward, we are falling behind. In earlier times, it was easier and more accepted to settle down in the stable comfort of one's social network. Now, we often have to fend for ourselves. A growing number of people lose their footing in this race due to insufficient psychological, social and/or economic resources.

The individualization trend is spreading to all aspects of society. To find a deeper explanation, I go back to Michel Foucault and his analysis of power discourse and subjectification. These reflections aim to shed light on the consequences of subjectification on the individual's identity development.

Power discourse and subjectification

Foucault's ideas about power resistance and subjectification continue to interest many social scientists, even, and especially, after Foucault's death. Heller[34] has made a valuable contribution by summarizing interpretations of Foucault's ideas in scholarly texts, which can be summed up as follows:

1   Subjects do not consciously exercise power but are merely subjected to power as passive objects.
2   Because subjects are shaped by power relations over which they have no control, subjectivity is shaped in a uniform and mechanical process. Consequently, a subversive subjectivity – which expresses itself in resistance to the system – cannot develop.
3   Power, from Foucault's perspective, is supreme and absolute. And resistance becomes a ubiquitous but fairly generalized – metaphysical – maxim.
4   Because power relations are the dominant principle in Foucault's analysis, it is difficult to imagine the possibility of escaping from this power. By implication, that would make society a fairly unpleasant experience.

---

34 Heller, K. J. (1996). Power, subjectification and resistance in Foucault. *SubStance*, 25, 1, 78–110.

Today, power is rarely represented by an external control agency, a dictator, a boss or similar, who is able to order people around. Power is expressed differently today. Power is an immanent aspect of the discourse. In the present context, discourse refers to systems of meaning where concepts, understandings, knowledge and actions are ordered in certain specific ways that are accepted in the social space, and which are themselves involved in shaping the context. The discursive power is near-invisible and thus difficult to grasp – or seize. Power is expressed via language and acts in the way the subject relates to self and others. And it is precisely through this subjectification that power unfolds its discursive agency: the individuals themselves have, in a sense, internalized the discourse and act accordingly. The subject exercises *self-monitoring*: am I doing okay? Am I okay? How might I do more to live up to others' demands and expectations – and my own ambitions? What (more) can I do to keep up with my classmate, my neighbour, my co-worker – or to do better? Discursive power expresses itself in the individual through *self-monitoring* and *self-control*. We do not need a strong sovereign. We keep ourselves in check.

Discursive power is hard to escape. It constitutes a ubiquitous, determining factor that influences our self-concept, our identity development, the way we act towards others and the way in which we treat ourselves. The German-Korean philosopher Han speaks of *smart power*, which 'cosies up to the psyche rather than disciplining it through coercion or prohibitions'. The 'Like' button is its *signum*. We voluntarily bow down to a power constellation while we communicate or consume.[35] Identity always involves processes where the individual subject relates to the social environment; here, however, this pertains not only to concrete, significant others, but also to the discourse and the power constellation that Foucault and Han discuss, each in their way. The big question now is how to address the discourse and smart power when it is almost invisibly enmeshed in the way in which we all act and communicate? Can we preserve and, perhaps, realize our dreams of the good life?

Utopian dreams of authenticity

Over the past decade or so, certain concepts have emerged, perhaps mainly as reflections of our dream of finding ourselves, reaching out to others and building a life that is harmonious and balanced. The term *authenticity* has manifested itself in our social life,[36] in organizations and as a personal and management ideal. The word *authentic* comes from the Greek *authentikos* (original, genuine, principal) and from *authentes* (acting on one's own authority).[37] I have previously described authenticity as:

---

35 Han (2017). *Psychopolitics*, pp. 12 ff.
36 See, for example, pop sociologist E. van Hauen: www.femina.dk/dit-liv/selvudvikling/er-du-autentisk.
37 See *authentic* at www.etymonline.com.

a personal experience of one's own stance, attitude and being, which in others' perception and approval of this state is perceived as directly proportional to one's own level of reflection, that is, the more aware one is of one's own feelings and intentions in relation to others, the more authentic is one able to be.[38]

In our current society, where power is so invisible and persistent as a general discourse – at last, in Foucault's and Han's thinking – we strive *to be authentic*. It becomes, unsurprisingly, a dream for anyone. As individuals, we wish to show others what we are about, and how we manage to live up to our own values and convictions. Authenticity is in high demand in management and leadership today, where the culture has a much greater emphasis on dialogue and interactions with the employees than it did in the past.[39]

However, authenticity contains a paradox that is not easy to dissolve; it lies in the tension between the person's basic position versus the conditions and demands of the social context, for example in an organization. In a management context, Herminia Ibarra has clarified the paradox in an article in the *Harvard Business Review*.[40] This paradox puts the viability of the concept of authenticity in doubt. Ibarra describes a solution perspective that may overcome the authenticity paradox, but which also makes it necessary to abandon authenticity in its original sense: *the problem* arises if authenticity is seen as an immutable sense of self ('That's simply the way I am!'). That version of authenticity is an obstacle. We need to realize that our experiences change us, just as we change with the contexts and challenges we face. *The solution*, as Ibarra sees it, is to learn to experiment with our identity. We adapt and alter our behaviour and self-concept to match the current situation. The crucial point in her analysis: by adopting an exclusively adaptive approach we may feel that we are letting ourselves down. She points out, however, that we develop most when we are *outside our comfort zone*. Ibarra's reflections make it clear that authenticity requires more than a simplistic understanding. If we include Foucault's discourse theory and Han's point about smart power, authenticity becomes an almost impossible goal, because we are enmeshed in certain power discourses that fundamentally shape the way we act.

Heteroenticity – being with oneself through the other

In my mind, *the only* viable path is the *interpersonal path*: creating something new in and through the relationships we develop, nurture and live within. This is where we may attempt to create dialogue and shared and coordinated action –

---

38 Stelter (2014). *A Guide to Third Generation Coaching*, p. 206.
39 See, for example: Ladkin, D., & Spiller, Ch. (2013). *Authentic Leadership, Clashes, Convergences and Coalescences* (New horizons in leadership studies). Cheltenham: Edward Elgar.
40 *Harvard Business Review*, Jan.–Feb. 2015.

approaches where authenticity begins to emerge, but where it is the *meeting with the other* and *the qualitative, that is, co-creative format of the meeting* that enables us to meet ourselves as well as the other.

Narrative co-creative, meaning-making and value-oriented dialogues with inspiration from third-generation coaching can form the basis for this shortcut, which may transcend the individual dream of authenticity. In this, I am very inspired by the concept of *heteroenticity*, a term coined by Ole Fogh Kirkeby. Heteroenticity is the opposite of authenticity and is defined as or *relating to oneself through the other*.[41] Heteroenticity is the possible path that I dream of, and which also lives up to the fundamental challenges of identity formation in postmodern or late modern society, which requires the individual to juggle many different relationships in 'real' as well as virtual worlds. Heteroenticity lets us take identity development and self-development to a new qualitative level. By embracing heteroenticity the individual escapes the need to have to fend for him/herself all the time. We need to develop practice, interaction, collaboration and dialogue forms that do away with the limitation of considering development and responsibility as exclusively individual endeavours, rather than something that unfolds in a shared space.[42] In writing this book I have embarked on a journey of my own. I invite you, the reader, to engage in thinking with me and to develop new dialogue and practice approaches that enable you to make yourself available to the other and to engage in co-creating a shared and different reality. In crisis situations it becomes particularly crucial that we are able to create a free space and to remain open to and interested in the other.[43] Via open conversations with a clear agenda and direction, we can develop civic society and generate social capital in local communities and in organizations.

Closing remarks

Authenticity is a dream, where the individual hopes to discover the core of his or her identity. Today, a search for identity is a highly complex undertaking, however. We may experience moments when we feel a sense of authenticity by *being able to act on our own authority*. In most cases, however, we are mutually dependent, not fully autonomous. At the same time, compromise may not always be the right answer, because they seem to require us to give up too much of

---

41 Kirkeby, O. F. (2009). *The New Protreptics – the Concept and the Art.* Copenhagen: Copenhagen Business School Press, pp. 101, 131. In Greek 'hetero' means 'the other' and '*einai=to be*'.
42 Similar ideas are reflected in the term 'holagracy', where the organization's hierarchical management structure is dissolved, and a social governance system is introduced throughout the organization via smaller, self-organizing groups. See more at https://en.wikipedia.org/wiki/Holacracy.
43 I see a promising initiative in borgerlyst.dk and medborgerne.dk. See also Lloyd, A. & Pass, N. (2015). *Samtalesaloner – små skub, der får folk til at falde i snak.* (Self-published via http://borgerlyst.dk/webshop) See also pp. 124–127 in this book.

ourselves. Authority can emerge from a community when we co-create something (new), where the individual members of the community recognize their own ideals, dreams and core values. The path forward is to make oneself available to other or to invite the other into a space of reflection and dialogue that has room for us both. This space should be one that we co-create. And that is exactly what third-generation coaching and other forms of fruitful and transformative dialogues are about: co-creating a shared space for reflection, where the individual and anyone else who is involved can change and develop: 'In dialogue both sides are willing to change'.[44]

---

44 This quote by Thich Nhat Hanh is the motto of my book *Third Generation Coaching*. In his book *The Art of Communicating* from 2013 Hanh has several interesting reflections on dialogue format and the dialogue guide's attitude to his or her dialogue partner.

Part II

Basic themes of fruitful dialogues

In Part II, I introduce three key themes that form the basis of fruitful dialogues and third-generation coaching. The themes frame interpersonal interactions and enable the individual to meet him/herself through others. The three themes are presented separately, strictly for purposes of analysis and to enable an in-depth examination of each one. However, they are inextricably interwoven. Each theme highlights a basic aspect of the content that forms the substance of the dialogue. As their interconnectedness can make it difficult to keep them apart in the following, my presentation therefore also points out the clear links connecting them.

The first theme is *the meaning-making* through the dialogue as a basis of understanding and coherence in any process of communication and reflection, both to the individual's self-reflection and to the community in the social context. I present personal and social meaning-making as pillars of fruitful dialogues. In the theoretical presentation I seek to integrate a phenomenological-existential and perceptual perspective with a social-constructionist and co-creative one.

The next theme is *values* as an essential foundation shaping the actions of individual as well as social communities in a given context. I highlight values as an event-sense and a condition for taking action. They define our implicit agency. Values thus help give the subject a sense of existential security and connectedness in the situation.

The third theme is *narratives* as the human way of finding meaning and expressing core values. It is through narratives we create meaning. It is through stories that our values unfold and connect with everyday situations. It is by finding new ways of speaking about oneself with another that we shape new narratives and thus lay a foundation for transformation and development, on an individual or community basis.

These three themes should be understood as a necessary theoretical basis and guidelines for creating a new dialogue culture. The dialogue guide's or coach's key question is: 'How do I generate meaning, explore values and formulate and reformulate narratives in the dialogue?' As the reader, you probably, and rightly so, would like to see a clear methodology or guideline for how you can develop your own skills as a third-generation coach or as an initiator of and partner in fruitful transformative dialogues. In Part II, I therefore examine and outline how these theoretically anchored basic themes can unfold in practice in the concrete relationship between the dialogue partners.

Chapter 4
Meaning-making in dialogue

Meaning-making is an existential premise for individuals' self-understanding and for social interactions.[1] I revisit here the concept of 'meaning', which I have long considered one of the most essential theoretical components of third-generation coaching. Finding what is meaningful in specific situations, through our actions and in life in general is a fundamental basis of human viability. I examine the concept from an etymological perspective in order to discover how meaning-making has come to play such an important role in our life: where does the term come from, and what are the most important related concepts?

I examine meaning as a key concept and as a basis for being able to linger in the dialogue and thus experience a more profound understanding of oneself, one's life and one's surroundings. Meaning emerges through two separate and, in practice, intertwined processes: through a bodily-sensory immersion in the situation and through relational interactions in dialogue. Building on the link between existential-phenomenological and social-constructionist-co-creative theory I develop an approach that enables fruitful and transformative dialogues (for example, coaching, mentoring and everyday professional conversations) that integrate meaning as a key pillar of this dialogue practice.

Striving for meaning and a personal existential foundation

In previous chapters I have examined how our society is characterized by an excess of information and constant demands on the individual to deal with people and relationships as well as other input that increasingly reaches us via digital media. The vast number of contacts and updates we encounter on a daily basis makes it increasingly necessary for us to be able to make sense of it all in a way that enables a stable and coherent perception of both self and environment.

Over the past decade I have noticed a search, both in the general public and in individuals, for an outlook that focuses on *existential meaning*. This is manifest

---

1 My first publication in the field of coaching psychology was: Stelter, R. (2007). Coaching: A process of personal and social meaning making. *International Coaching Psychology Review*, 2(2), 191–201.

both in a growing radicalization (sectarian fundamentalism) and – on a more constructive note – in a renaissance of existential topics, including an interest in existential philosophy[2] and a search for authenticity and self-awareness, for example via mindfulness, meditation, wellness, body awareness, yoga and a greater emphasis on the body in general. The significant attention to the self-improvement craze that was earned by Brinkmann's book *Stand Firm* – first in Denmark and now internationally – is probably also a sign of a general shift in the population. Ultimately, this search for a personal existential foundation should also be seen as an indication of the basic direction that coaching and other professional everyday dialogues should pursue: developing *the art of lingering in dialogue* as a way to find meaning and a personal existential foundation in one's personal and working life.

In connection with this quest for *existential meaning*, a reflective dialogue practitioner or coach may consider whether systemic and social-constructionist theories can still meet all the needs with regard to describing, explaining and influencing social (change) processes. Systemic and social-constructionist theories, which have been developed in an attempt to explain and act in a field of growing complexity and the individual's many contacts and interactions, continue to play an important role in addressing and understanding relational, structural and performative processes in society. Moreover, these theories underpin practice-oriented support and consultancy through the use of relational and collaborative models.[3] As described in the discussion of identity in Chapter 3, the self is shaped by the relationships each of us is a part of and is influenced by. Systemic and social-constructionist theories emerged precisely to meet the need to explain and influence complex social processes in late-modern and postmodern society. On a positive note, I would like to highlight the usefulness and applicability of these theories in a wide range of organizational contexts. However, there does appear to be a need to bring in additional theories to capture individuals' growing needs for a personal existential foundation orientation.

It is not, however, my intention to revert to an individualizing, egocentric perspective. Although I do wish to address the new, justified needs of the individual, I also strive to include the other as a partner in shaping and enabling an understanding of the individual's reality and in building communities where the mutual facilitation of personal development can become a key element. Here, I would remind the reader of the concept of *heteroenticity – relating to oneself through the other* – as fundamental to my understanding (cf. Chapter 3).

---

2 The celebration of the bicentenary of Kierkegaard's birth in 2013 may have offered an occasion to highlight existential concerns. However, there is probably a deeper explanation for the renaissance of existential topics that can be explored in the changes in society and the demands to self and identity, as described in the closing chapters of the present book.
3 See, for example, Haslebo, G. (2004). *Relationer i organisationer.* Copenhagen: Dansk Psykologisk Forlag; Haslebo, G. & Lund, G. E. (2014). *Relationsudvikling i Skolen.* Copenhagen: Dansk Psykologisk Forlag.

Meaning as the top level in the hierarchy of intentionality

A search for meaning, which always involves a focus on values, is a search for a personal existential foundation and whatever makes our lives and our actions meaningful. Previously in the present book, I have expressed my disinclination to focus exclusively or excessively on specific goals or problems, which is the basic perspective in first-generation coaching, where the coach helps the focus person get from point A to point B. The coaching literature in general contains growing criticism of such a narrow goal perspective.[4] Goals and objectives can lock a person into a particular societal discourse; this, ultimately, represents the polar opposite of the purpose of a good dialogue (cf. Chapter 2), which is to enable novel perspectives. Furthermore, the goal focus often changes during the coaching process,[5] precisely because the participants in the dialogue embark on a reflective process that brings deeper layers to light and consequently changes the dialogue partner's perspective and interests. To highlight this aspect, I introduce the following model of the hierarchy of intentionality (Figure 4.1), which positions meaning at the top level.[6]

The model operates with three levels:

- *Meaning*: This is the most abstract and the overarching level. It addresses the meaningful, which is often rooted in certain narratives or unfolded when we

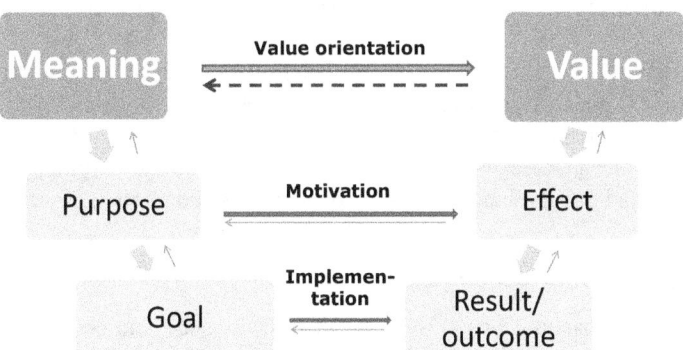

Figure 4.1 Meaning as the highest positioned in the hierarchy of intentionality[7] (the dotted line suggests the ambition of protreptics, which revolves around values. Read more about this aspect in Chapter 5).

---

4 David, S., Clutterbuck, D., & Megginson, D. (eds.) (2013). *Beyond Goals – Effective Strategies for Coaching And Mentoring*. Farnham: Gower.
5 See more in Ordóñez, L. D., Schweitzer, M. E., Galinsky, A. E. & Bazerman, M. H. (2009). Goals gone wild: the systematic side effects of overprescribing goal setting. *Academy of Management Perspectives*, 23, 1, 6–16.
6 The model was first presented in a coaching context in Stelter, R. (2009). *Coaching as a Reflective Space* and has been reused repeatedly, not least in Stelter, R. (2014). *Third Generation Coaching*.
7 The model was originally presented by the German action theorist and Professor of Sport Psychology Jürgen Nitsch (1986). I have used the model in connection with coaching (see, for example, Stelter, 2012).

immerse ourselves in a bodily-sensory examination of certain specific situations and events. At the meaning level, we also explore the core values for our way of being in the world. A protreptic dialogue would take the opposite approach; it begins with core concepts and values (such as courage, agency, freedom) and examines them in a general, non-situation-specific way. The purpose is to develop an event-sense and a capacity to act for situations the person encounters (for example, a director who needs to show agency). A certain action is seen in the larger context. Questions at this level could include, for example, 'What does it mean for me to meet new people?' or 'What meaning does winning hold for me?'.

- *Purpose*: Here, the outcome of a series of events with a particular effect and a desired purpose. The actor asks about the effect, for example, 'What do I want to achieve with my stamina training?' or 'What purpose does the conversation with XY have for me (and for XY)?'. This is the most obvious level on which to locate the actual motivation process.
- *Goal*: Actions are oriented towards a specific goal. The actor is more or less focused on the outcome, for example, 'I want to lose 20 kg!' (see description of Anna's case later in this chapter).

Thus, for every act, the person asks certain questions about the meaning, purpose and goal of engaging with his or her environment. These questions are answered within the framework of value, purpose and goal hierarchies. Thus, the action theory perspective that frames this model is not aimed at finding causal explanations, but instead at examining intentions and at positioning the action in the person's concrete environmental and existential context. To be able to linger in dialogue, one has to move away from a narrow goal focus by exploring meaning and values and thus seeking a deeper understanding of oneself and one's world.

Finding meaning through coaching

At its origins, coaching was closely associated with sport and performance optimization. It often aimed at helping the individual to realize his or her full potential, to strive for and attain his or her goal. In the literature, this narrow focus on goals and on clearly defined problems as the key perspective of coaching is viewed with increasing criticism, as mentioned earlier. A narrow goal focus is short term and does not ensure a sustainable dialogue in the long term. Besides, the goals have been found to change during the coaching process.[8] This has necessitated a broader approach to coaching that addresses the purpose and meaning of coaching

---

8 Cf. Ordóñez, L. D., Schweitzer, M. E., Galinsky, A. E. & Bazerman, M. H. (2009). Goals gone wild: The systematic side effects of overprescribing goal setting. *Academy of Management Perspectives*, 23(1), 6–16.

in relation to certain activities and life situations. Organization scholars Weick and Sutcliffe[9] observe a tendency towards mindlessness, which they describe as a form of mental activity where people simply follow manuals, rely on obsolete categories, act with rigidity or operate on auto-pilot. They argue that the world is too complex to predict development processes on the basis of narrowly defined goals.

This criticism against the traditional linear thinking of coaching (as represented, for example, by first-generation coaching) has inspired a further development of the field. Second-generation coaching and certain systemically inspired organization development strategies aim for a broader perspective by examining the dialogue partner's potential strengths in given situations and by exploring dynamics that promote cooperation. These methods explore potential solutions that lie hidden in certain contexts. In third-generation coaching the dialogue guide acts as a co-reflective partner. Here, the aim is to create moments of symmetry in the dialogue. The dialogue seeks to enhance both interlocutors' capacity to reflect: helping to *clarify the other's personal and social meaning* is the main task for the dialogue guide (coach). The ultimate goal in a narrative co-creative process is to enhance the interlocutors' reflective capacity and sense of self-identity and thus their sense of coherence, in part by discovering the link between past and present events and integrating them into a potential future perspective.

Based on earlier empirical and theoretical studies,[10] complexity theorist Stacey recommends a 'conversational, reflexive narrative inquiry'.[11] This term may pertain to many transformative and fruitful dialogue forms, including third-generation coaching, and thus offers an alternative to the restrictive rules and procedures (for example in the highly goal-driven GROW model[12]). Considering the growing complexity in all aspects of life, we need new and more reflective dialogue forms and development strategies. More than ever, we have to live with the risk of misjudgement and faulty anzlyses. One strategy for how to deal with the permanent space of reflection would be deliberately to adopt a metaposition, that is, a reflective and curious stance to one's own self-reflexivity. Here, transformative and fruitful dialogues, inspired by third-generation coaching, play an important role in our search for and discovery of meaning.

---

9 Weick, K. E. & Sutcliffe, K. M. (2015). *Managing the Unexpected* (3rd edition). San Francisco: Jossey-Bass.
10 Stacey, R. D. (2001). *Complex Responsive Processes in Organizations: Learning and Knowledge Creation*. London: Routledge.
11 Stacey, R. D. (2012). Comment on debate article: Coaching psychology coming of age: The challenges we face in the messy world of complexity. *International Coaching Psychology Review*, 7(1) 91–95.
12 See, for example, Alexander, G. (2010). Behavioural coaching – the GROW– model. In Passmore, J. *Excellence in coaching: the industry guide* (2nd ed.). London; Philadelphia: Kogan. pp. 83–93.

Meaning – a closer look at the concept

Albert Einstein wrote,[13] 'The man who regards his own life and that of his fellow-creatures as meaningless is not merely unfortunate but almost disqualified for life'. Meaning-making is a fundamental requirement for the individual human being and for human communities, enabling us to find a position and a direction in key situations, and in life overall. Meaning-making is what makes humanity viable. In order to create a basic understanding of the concept of *meaning* and its depth, I will examine the origins of the word and compare it to related terms in order to uncover the meaning we intuitively associate with the word in our (Western) culture. Meaning stems from low-German word *meninge* and is explained with reference to words such as 'sense, import, intent'.[14] The word 'intent' implies a clear action dimension: by acting, we *find meaning* and *make sense* of the world. The German word *Sinn* is closely related to the concept of meaning. The German *Sinn* comes from Latin *sensus*: 'perceive, feel, know' and the proto-Indo-European *sent*: to give or take a certain direction.[15] Thus, if the individual imparts his or her action with a specific direction, meaning arises and unfolds. We impart direction through the way we act, how we talk about events and ourselves and the way we relate to others in our social environment. However, when we speak about imparting direction, it implies an underlying intention that may, similarly, vary and develop in the course of the process. Thus, meaning is something we create in dialogue with our material and social environment through a certain *relationship of meaning* that we create or choose.

Meaning in an existential and phenomenological perspective

Viktor E. Frankl was a professor of neurology and psychiatry. He was interred during the Second World War in several Nazi concentration camps, but he survived the madness and went on to have a long career before his death in 1997. Frankl described an important basis for our understanding of *meaning* after studying the concept intensely after escaping the camps where he had to find a sense of meaning to survive the insanity of his cruel incarceration. Based on phenomenological theory, Frankl's book *The Will to Meaning*[16] propose *Finding and Fulfilling Meaning* as the basic striving of a human being. Meaning takes form in the individual's active interaction with his or her surroundings, which is what brings substance to our lives. According to gestalt psychologist Max Wertheimer, any life situation contains an invitation to act, which constitutes

---

13 Einstein, A. (2007). *The World As I See It*. San Diego, CA: The Booktree, p. 1.
14 See *Online Etymology Dictonary* www.etymonline.com.
15 See German etymological dictionary at www.dwds.de/?view=1&qu=Sinn [accessed 23 November 2015) and www.etymonline.com (look up mean[ing] and sense).
16 Frankl, V. E. (1988). *The Will to Meaning. Foundations and Applications of Logotherapy*. New York, NY: New American Library. (German original from 1978).

the meaning of the situation. The individual imbues his environment with specific meaning in any given situation. In this interaction between the person and the situation the person searches for meaning. In accordance with phenomenology Frankl speaks of the will to meaning and posits the following basic assumption: as conscious beings, humans will always search for meaning. Frankl sees three ways of finding meaning: first of all, human beings discover meaning by *creating or doing something*; next, we find meaning by *experiencing something* or *encountering someone*; and finally, when we are in a situation without hope, where we feel helpless, we do it by *choosing to search for meaning*. The key in the latter situation is the attitude by which we meet our unavoidable suffering.[17] Based on this, Frankl proposes a typology of values with the following three elements:

1 Creative values.
2 Experiential values.
3 Attitudinal values.

Frankl's description and categories illustrate the close link between meaning-making and values.

Meaning in a systemic and social-constructionist perspective

In the systemic and social-constructionist universe, the understanding of meaning is removed from the individual's life universe. *In systemic theory*, meaning arises when a particular pattern develops as the result of certain feedback mechanisms, for example between two persons: the boss puts down virtually everything the employee proposes, and the employee becomes increasingly insecure and nervous about doing the right thing. In this understanding, meaning reflects a pattern in the social or organizational field. Meaning is a dynamic concept that can only be understood from a specific observer perspective. The actual patterns may sometimes be difficult for the involved parties themselves to discern.[18]

Social-constructionist thinkers are very interested in the dynamic that develops *between* the actors, as they *co-create* their shared reality.[19] Here, meaning is understood from a relational perspective. Meaning-making takes place in the

---

17 Ibid.
18 A good description of various feedback mechanisms and their consequences for relational patterns is found in Bertelsen, M. & Ejlersen, S. (2005). Teamudvikling i relationen. In R. Stelter & M. Bertelsen, *Team – Udvikling og Læring*. Virum: Dansk Psykologisk Forlag. For a new article on destructive and strengthening feedback patterns, see Wulff, D., St. George, S., Tomm, K., Doyle, E. & Sesma, M. (2015). Unpacking the PIPs to HIPs curiosity: A narrative study. *Journal of Systemic Therapies*. 34(2), 45–58.
19 See more in Gergen, K. J. (1994). *Realities and Relationships*. 2nd edition. Boston, MA: Harvard University Press.

dialogue. It arises through the relationship and in the context of the dialogue. If the dialogue partner follows up with a comment or a statement, he or she coordinates this utterance with others, thus framing it as a form of follow-up (speech) act. In a social-constructionist understanding the individual does not generate meaning alone; meaning is shaped, developed and reframed continually during the conversation. Their universe of meaning is co-created in the course of the conversation, which thus always results in something new for both parties, something that emerges in the mutual meeting, which they could not have arrived at on their own, without speaking to one another.

These two dimensions and processes of meaning-making – the phenomenological existential and the social-constructionist relational – I typically view as integrated, as part of the way in which we shape our lives. They are the theoretical foundation for the dialogue.

Two processes of meaning-making

Meaning-making is an integration of individual and sociocultural processes.[20] The dialogue guide can draw on this theoretical distinction in practice: first, by positioning him/herself in the dialogue partner's universe of meaning, that is, by understanding the other, and later with a view to extend, change and reinterpret the dialogue partner's – and ultimately his or her own – horizon of meaning.

In the following, I draw an analytical distinction between two lines of meaning-making, which in practice tend to fuse into one in the actual dialogue:

1 *Phenomenological and existential processes*: Meaning is found through experiences and (implicit) knowledge that the individual forms in a variety of situations and events. In this process, individuals attain some degree of awareness of their concrete and sensory connection to the world. They develop meaning by acting in specific sociocultural and material contexts. The 'outer' world becomes real and meaningful through the sensory reflection that occurs in a dialogue or a coaching conversation focused on a certain event. From a phenomenological point of view, meaning emerges in an interplay between one's experience and the way it is perceived and interpreted. Through our concrete actions we develop a *sensory and thus a meaningful relationship* with our environment. Thus, the environment is not a phenomenon that can be accessed objectively, but something that is created in the relationship between the individual and the specific situation that forms the context. Initially, this meaning relationship emerges through a vague sensation that is hard to capture in words. Within a supportive dialogue, the best way

---

20 These considerations have been previously described in Stelter (2014). *Third Generation Coaching* and in several articles, including Stelter (2012). Stelter, R. (2014). Third generation coaching: reconstructing dialogues through collaborative practice and a focus on values. International Coaching Psychology Review, 9, 1, 33-48.

to capture this sensation verbally is often by means of a metaphor that puts the individual's subjectively perceived reality into words. Meaning can also be conveyed by other means, such as drawings, bodily expressions or dance or by written or spoken words that do not involve metaphors. By highlighting and making room for experiential meaning the dialogue guide helps the dialogue partner develop a greater experiential and existential understanding of him/herself and of the cultural and social context that he or she lives in. This dialogue primarily revolves around bodily and sensory aspects. It deals with sensations, where the dialogue guide seeks to grasp the dialogue partner's life world by developing a sense of what is at stake for the other. This is where the phenomenological and existentialist perspective is unfolded in practice. Together with the dialogue guide, the dialogue partner seeks to understand his or her subjective reality or experiences within the given culture and context. The focus is on the implicit and often bodily sensory dimensions of certain situations, actions or persons. This perspective can help shed light on essential and existentially meaningful experiences and values associated with past events – with an emphasis on uplifting moments – and on what one perceives as genuine and important. In this process, the dialogue should strive to uncover the practices, habits and routines that are embedded in the flow of the action. An in-depth examination of the actual practice, a sensory reliving of it, will often be a source of new insight for the dialogue partner. Things that are simply 'what I normally do', without much conscious attention, should be explored to uncover the underlying meaning and thus enhance the person's self-awareness. The dialogue guide aims to initiate a process that gives the dialogue partner a chance to develop a sensory experience of a specific situation or event. Only once it has been articulated is the experience unfolded as an important aspect of the event and thus attributed meaning for the person. In the phenomenologically inspired literature[21] the *felt sense* of a situation is mentioned as key to developing a verbal grasp of the experience. When experiences take centre stage in the dialogue, the dialogue partner can develop a sense of him/herself as an actor that explores his or her own actions from a sensory perspective, reliving important aspects of the situation that had been forgotten as part of the person's tacit knowledge.

2   *Social-constructionist relational processes*: The second key aspect of co-creative dialogues is the understanding of meaning as a co-creative and collaborative process driven by both dialogue participants. Kenneth Gergen describes it as follows:

---

21 Gendlin, E. T. (1996). *Focusing-Oriented Psychotherapy*. New York/London: The Guilford Press; Gendlin, E. T. (1997). *Experiencing and the Creation of Meaning*. Evanston, IL: Northwestern University Press (original from 1962); Gendlin, E. T. (1982). *Focusing* (2nd edition). New York, NY: Bantam Books; Stelter, R. (2010). Experience-based and body-anchored qualitative interviewing. *Qualitative Health Research*, 20(6), 859–867.

There is an alternative way of approaching the problem of social meaning: removing the individual as the starting point opens a range of promising possibilities. Rather than commence with individual subjectivity and work deductively toward an account of human understanding through language, we may being our analysis at the level of the *human relationship* as it generates both language and understanding.[22]

Meaning is thus negotiated by the participants within a specific social setting or community of practice – a team, a school class, a department, a sports team or a dialogue between two or more persons (for example in a coaching process). Here, the focus of the conversation shifts away from individual experiences and sensations towards the community, the relationships and the context. In this setting, reality is generated in the social setting through the way we act *together* and the way we *speak with each other*. The way in which we make ourselves available to the other, and the way we interact, in actions and language, influence our understanding of ourselves and each other. You are involved in shaping reality for the other. The other is involved in shaping your reality. Reality is thus a co-production, jointly shaped by everyone involved.

In the dialogue practice that may take the following form: the dialogue partner presents a certain perception of his or her reality, generated outside the dialogue space, through the relationships that the dialogue partner engages in at work, at home, in leisure activities or in other life contexts. The dialogue guide may offer one new voice among the actors that the dialogue partner hears and has to deal with. In the actual conversation, the dialogue guide may become a key voice in the dialogue partner's new process of meaning-making, because the conversation constitutes a new, actively chosen context, where the dialogue partner is looking for new impulses to supplement his or her current perspective. The dialogue guide's task is to support the other's reflections on the cultural roots and social relations that might influence the dialogue partner's self-perception and perception of his or her social reality. With inspiration from third-generation coaching the dialogue guide also become a co-reflective partner, who offers his or her own understanding, reflections and way of being touched and affected by what the dialogue partner says. This sensitive and empathic participation in the conversation changes both participants, who thus become participants in the joint meaning-making process that draws on individual experiences and highlights the reality, the relationships, the culture and the contexts that they are both part of. These thoughts about co-creative meaning-making are revisited in the possible joint reflection on certain values (Chapter 5) and in narrative theory and practice (Chapter 6). The co-creation process as a dialogue practice is revisited in Chapter 8.

---

22 Gergen, K. J. (2005), *Realities and Relationships*. (2nd edition). Boston, MA: Harvard University Press, p. 263.

Intentionality and agency as the basis of meaning-making

As mentioned in the discussion about the etymological roots of the terms, *meaning* and *sense* both have an *intentional* dimension. Meaning emerges when we choose a *direction* through our actions. Intentionality, our proactive orientation towards our environment, is a foundation stone in the understanding of human meaning-making processes. As a dimension of a theory of knowledge, the term *intentionality* is subject to debate, however.[23] Systems theorists and social-constructionists are wary of the concepts of personal *volition*, *intentionality* and *personal agency*.[24] That human beings have an inner drive and thus a responsibility for our own actions has been a core assumption in Western thinking since the Age of the Enlightenment (voluntarism: the notion of free will). Holding human beings personally responsible for their actions lays the foundation for morals and ethics in society. This thinking is also the basis of our legal system. We are held accountable for our actions. A causal logic is established between the perpetrator and the crime. The leading social-constructionist Kenneth Gergen argues that the *relationship* is the key 'driver' of action[25] – he regards *agency* as something that emerges in the relationship. As I read Gergen, even he has difficulty completely rejecting intentionality as a reflection of the individual's orientation towards the environment. Personal 'agency' is a deeply entrenched assumption in our (Western) culture. Within the relationship we also express a certain orientation towards the other, for example by showing appreciative interest, support or animosity. However, Gergen proposes a view of 'agency' as a *product of the relationship* as a way of proposing a new, fresh perspective. This 'co-creative agency' is Gergen's invitation to another way of being together that offers to give rise to new understandings of joint agency. Participating in certain new relationships and practice communities can give rise to new ways of thinking and acting. In this sense, intentionality becomes a product of the relationship.

I choose to maintain a dual individual *and* relational perspective on the concept of intentionality:

1 Personal intention and volition can be what enables the individual to move, to take the initiative for a change, especially after the dialogue guide has invited the dialogue partner to engage in a sensory exploration of certain situations. This exploration often leads to a new self-concept in the context of the situation (cf. the case story about Anna below).
2 Often, this volition springs from the relationships we are a part of. Certain relationships or communities shape a certain understanding of certain persons,

---

23 I have previously described and discussed the concept of intentionality, in Stelter (2014). *Third Generation Coaching*. Some repetition is inevitable.
24 See Gergen, K. J. (2009). *Relational Being. Beyond Self and Community*. Oxford: Oxford University Press, p. 74.
25 See, especially in Gergen, K. J. (2009). *Relational Being. Beyond Self and Community*. Oxford: Oxford University Press, pp. 99–121.

situations, activities and so forth and attribute certain meaning to them. Certain phenomena are framed by a certain culture and discourse. Within certain communities/relationship, it can be almost impossible for the individual to break a fixed pattern. In that case, it is only by entering into a new community/relationship that the person can achieve development and change on a personal level – the volition that is now possible is an implicit part of the new context. In the case story below, my coaching conversations with Anna, helped her reinterpret herself and her life.

Coaching process with Anna

I was a coach for Anna, who contacted me because she wanted to lose weight.[26] She had tried a wide range of different diets and was tormented by her failure to achieve the change she desired. However, after participating in a workshop I held she saw an opportunity for working with herself – together with me – due to the approach to coaching that I presented. Undoubtedly, Anna had also previously possessed the determination and the desire to change her eating behaviour, but had failed to do so. Her personal determination simply was not strong enough. In my conversations with Anna we were able to co-create a new reality for her. Initially, we *explored the personal and sensory experiences related to the eating situation* (this part was guided mainly by the phenomenological approach): 'When you leave work: what do you do to prepare for your meal?' It emerged that she often worked late, and as a result she often resorted to picking up fast food and a fizzy drink from a nearby kiosk or fast-food restaurant. During the meal she was often reading on her computer. These descriptions of her subjective experiences revealed a pattern of behaviour. She began to notice that she never took the time to eat, that she did not appreciate the meal situation, that she was unaware of her eating habits, that she ate too fast and that she was not sufficiently mindful of what she was eating. During the ongoing dialogue process she also realized that she often overate at times when she felt stressed and insecure (due to pressures at work and uncertainty as to whether her job performance was good enough, and so forth). The many questions I asked helped her focus on implicit aspects of her eating habits and behaviours. That made it much easier for her to understand what was going on.

Although my contributions revolved around Anna's experiences I also engaged in *active withness thinking* and acted as a *co-reflective partner* during the dialogue. As a co-reflective partner I offered my own reflections on my perception of some of the situations she described. Without taking over the conversation, I served as a sounding board for her own thoughts and feelings. This gave rise to a practice

---

26 Read more about the case in Stelter, R. (2015). 'I tried so many diets, now I want to do it differently' – A single case study on coaching for weight loss. *International Journal of Qualitative Studies on Health and Well-Being*, 10: 26925; open access via: www.ijqhw.net/index.php/qhw/article/view/26925.

community between Anna and myself, which gave rise to new perspectives on her behaviour. Her sense of personal inadequacy and lack of willpower gradually began to change. Suddenly she saw a possibility for change. Her intention and determination grew with the growing understanding she developed as a result of our conversations. This new intentional orientation in Anna may be understood as a consequence of the discourse that she and I co-created. To quote Gergen:[27] 'Meaning is born in the coordination'. The new meaning that emerged, which led to a shift in Anna's attitude and the development of new eating habits, was the product of the coordination between my questions, her descriptions and reflections and my co-reflection. Ultimately, this coordination supported Anna's determination and ambition to do something else. That determination was facilitated by my presence, my empathy and my co-reflection in the dialogue. The new meaning that unfolded for Anna was expressed in one of her closing comments: 'It's not a diet, it's my life!'

That statement captures a new universe of meaning that unfolded for Anna based on the course of our dialogue. It is *not the objective* of weight loss that paves the way for change. She had this as her objective for years. It is *her new understanding of her entire life* in regard to food and eating, which was placed into a new context of meaning and thus enabled Anna's new behaviour. This coordination is also based on our individual intentions and our desire to build a relationship. When I wish the best for Anna, this shapes the relationship accordingly. Meaning is embedded in the act. Thus, the intention behind the relationship (for example to wish the best for the other) is expressed throughout the course of the relationship, and the developing relationship in turn enhances that meaning-making.

Maintaining a dual perspective of intentionality

Intentionality is the basis of the way we act. It is the basis of our capacity for meaning-making, both individually and together. In the narrative approach, intentionality is addressed in the concept of the *landscape of identity*, which is always linked with the *landscape of action* (see Chapter 6). The convictions, attitudes, values and so forth that spring from our identity unfold in the landscape of identity and have a crucial influence on our actions in the world. That is why Anna says that the core issue is not a diet, but her life. This new self-perception enables her to act in a new way that is more appropriate for her.

We care how the people around us react to our actions. Thus, the *relationship* has a crucial impact on who we are, and who we become. I have described these processes as being *social-constructionist* and *relational*. This topic is revisited in the discussion of the narrative universe in Chapter 6, where I highlight the

---

27 Gergen, K. J. (2009). *Relational Being. Beyond Self and Community*. Oxford: Oxford University Press, p. 74.

co-creative dialogue form as a proactive use of the relational interaction in a community of practice for meaning-making.

In addition to the relational concept of identity I maintain the phenomenological concept of *operative intentionality*.[28] In relating to their environment, individuals take an intentional and fundamentally bodily stance. This sensory-aesthetic involvement with the situation via the body is unfolded in the dialogue as a fundamental basis of the individual's *being in the world*. Through a sensory focus the dialogue guide can support the dialogue partner, and in this way both participants approach a deeper understanding of the dialogue partner's life world. Merleau-Ponty introduced and established an understanding of the body as a 'sensory organ'; it is in this sense that the body, via perception and action, relates to the specific contextual situation.[29] Merleau-Ponty's notion of the intentional orientation of the perceptions/sensory impressions is key to our understanding of pre-reflective knowledge as something that is given and immediately available in the situation. The mind 'reaches out' to the environment, and sensations and actions are interconnected in a circular loop: I am involved in the situation; I am sensorily guided by my immediate involvement and actions in the situation; I am in the situation via my pre-reflective intentionality, which is sensorily rooted in practice and context; I do not reflect on cognitive rules and strategies that might constrain my actions; events unfold as I act; my action is based on spontaneous, nonverbalized knowledge; I know how to proceed; my actions are a part of my sensorimotor habits. This implicit, habitual practice in particular can become the starting point of a dialogue. Here, the dialogue partner needs empathic support from a dialogue guide who is able – in cooperation with the dialogue partner in a close, empathic process – to put the implicit practice into words.

Closing remarks

By focusing on meaning the dialogue guide can add intensity to the conversation. One way of doing that is by inviting the dialogue partner to explore specific situations and events. Meaning is reshaped in the participants' relational interaction in the dialogue; meaning is thus a result of the co-creative practice that frames the conversation.

Finding meaning is the essence of life, and it helps us understand ourselves, our lives and others in a new or 'better' way. In a world that is characterized by a high degree of complexity and growing diversification in many areas of society, interest communities and groups, and where individuals are pushed to pursue 'self-realization' and relentless self-improvement, the search for a personal

---

28 Cf. Freemann, A. (1994). Operative intentionality: Notes on Merleau-Ponty's approach to mental activities that are not the exclusive product of the conscious mind. *Journal of Phenomenological Research*, 24(1), 78–89.
29 Merleau-Ponty, M. (2012). *Phenomenology of Perception*. London: Routledge

existential foundation and meaning becomes an important personal task that should also be taken seriously in organizations, companies, schools, hospitals and other institutional settings. The search for meaning gives any kind of dialogue a profound foundation. The art of lingering in dialogue is a journey into the human universe of meaning.

Chapter 5

Values – a basis for action

Our current times promote a sense of restlessness where life is not always perceived as meaningful but instead often makes us slaves to self-control and our own performance drive. We have lost the art of lingering and fail to make time for reflection. Reflecting on values gives individuals a strong basis for being able to act. Values emerge when we immerse ourselves in what is meaningful and most important in our lives. Values also come to the forefront in conflict situations and acknowledged dilemma situations. Examining values or central concepts and themes helps prepare us to act with confidence, consistence and commitment. Values are a key anchor point for our identity and a link between our ethical convictions and our actions.

In this chapter I present various ethical positions developed by philosophers throughout history. Aristotle's situational ethics, which posits that individuals strive for good, can be seen as an approach to coaching and other professional and private everyday dialogues and forms one of the central pillars of the value-oriented understanding of dialogue in this book. In this chapter I describe how values can be defined and their specific impact on promoting a deeper dialogue.[1] In closing, I describe two approaches to value-oriented dialogues that spring from either a protreptic or a situation-specific point of departure. Despite the differences between these two perspectives, both approaches make it possible to focus on something that may prove valuable to both participants in the dialogue. Thus, reflecting on values leads to symmetrical and shared human moments in the dialogue.

The vita contemplativa

In a social critique the Korean-German philosopher Han[2] characterizes our everyday life as hyperactive. We live in a time when we have forgotten the art of lingering. A narrow focus on goals, a constant quest to move on and the fear

---

1 Similar ideas are presented in Stelter, R. (2016). Working with values in coaching. In T. Bachkirova, G. Spence, & D. Drake (eds.), *The SAGE Handbook of Coaching* (pp. 333–347). London: Sage Publications.

of missing out (FoMO) lead to a sense of restlessness, where life does not always appear meaningful, but often makes us slaves to our own self-control and performance drive. The growing tendency to self-monitor is further promoted via 'likes' and constant 'updates' from our 'friends' on social media. To be *our own masters* we need to pause, reflect and stop always striving for the next achievement. As a counterpoint to this trend Han reaches back to a concept from Heidegger, *Besinnung* – reflective thought – and the *vita contemplativa*. In order to find our way back to ourselves and regain our strength, we need to be able to linger – on our own, with a coach, with a colleague, with a friend or in a group of people who share this desire. Only when we linger in our thoughts and speak with calm reflection can we spend time together in a way that is experienced as rewarding, refreshing and fruitful (see, for example, my description of the conversation salon in Chapter 10). By pausing, reflecting and allowing our thoughts to unfold, we can learn to be present in the moment, both when we are with each other and in our own individual lives. To quote Han:[3] 'If language is deprived of what is indirect in it, its nature approaches that of a scream or an order. Friendliness and politeness are also based on the circuitous and the indirect'. Nuance and time for reflection bring substance and value to our thoughts and speech.

The meaning of values – then and now

We can practice the *vita contemplativa* by examining the concepts or values that hold special value in our lives – often without us realizing it. Consider such concepts as community, friendship, empathy, agency, courage, freedom, fairness and so forth. Values are becoming a hot topic in the professional literature on management and leadership, coaching and other aspects of organizational and dialogue practice.[4] The new focus on value-driven processes comes from a growing awareness that life and work in our globalized world require each of us to have a firm footing in order to grasp and connect with qualities that are meaningful to us, on a personal as well as social level. Organizations, too, increasingly need to embrace a set of values that is not merely presented on the corporate website or posted in the lobby, but which are *lived* in the organization, permeating the actions of their leaders and employees and present as something that can be *experienced* by the outside world, including business partners and potential clients or customers. Thus, in my understanding, values are often referred to as

---

2   Han, B.-C. (2017). *The Scent of Time: A Philosophical Essay on the Art of Lingering*. Cambridge, UK: Polity Press.
3   Ibid., p. 109. See also Han, B. (2015). *The Burnout Society*. Redwood City: Stanford University Press.
4   See, for example, de Gennaro, I. (ed.) (2012).*Value Sources and Readings on a Key Concept of the Globalized World*. Leiden: BRILL; a master's degree in ethics and values in organizations at Aarhus University and similar degrees at other universities around the world, multiple books and consultancies on value-based leadership and a scientific journal dedicated to the topic of values: *Journal of Human Values* (since 1995) are additional indications of this trend.

a *mood* and as a certain attunement between people rather than as operationalized criteria as part of a so-called value-based leadership – which is not what I am taking about here. In an organizational context, 'mood' is referred to as the 'atmosphere' where colleagues and teams create something together. A growing number of management and leadership theorists argue that values and sense-making (meaning-making) can serve as an anchor and a guideline for the individual manager's (and employee's) behaviour. Thus, values can help keep the organization on course.[5] Crucially, the values need to be visibly reflected in the actions of managers/leaders and employees, translated into an organization-wide value-based culture.

In response to traditional psychology and its preoccupation with dysfunction and deficiencies, positive psychology[6] has attempted to set a new agenda by directing our attention to values, among other qualities, and their potential to form a new basis for our actions and, ultimately, generating greater well-being, resilience and happiness. The Values-In-Action Inventory of Strengths (VIA),[7] which features 24 character strengths and virtues, is based on six core values: wisdom and knowledge; courage; humanity and love; justice; temperance; transcendence. VIA is a tool that aims to draw attention to an individual's strengths and dispositions to engage optimally with the environment and with other people. Although in some situations, a positive outlook may contribute to human well-being, there is also a risk of a tyranny of *positivity*; a critical angle that has been put forth by the American journalist and writer Barbara Ehrenreich[8] and the Danish sociologist Rasmus Willig[9] as some of its main proponents. Based on Ehrenreich's own experiences as a cancer patient she warns that positivity can, ultimately, lead to self-reproach and isolation. This illustrates the risk of functionalizing values with a view to aligning people around a particular mindset and behaviour.

There is a broad and growing recognition in society that we cannot continue the same hectic lifestyle, which only leads to exhaustion, stress, depression and a sense of existential dissatisfaction. I am seeing a growing awareness in society of the importance of community, social bonds, empathy, reflection and existential issues. Some people are embracing a new outlook with different values, replacing FoMO with JoMO – the Joy of Missing Out[10] – by lingering and enjoying the moment.

---

5 See, for example, Stacey, R. D. (2012). *The Tools and Techniques of Leadership and Management. Meeting the Challenge of Complexity*. London: Routledge; Weick, K. E. (1995). *Sensemaking in Organizations*. Thousand Oaks, CA: Sage.
6 See Lopez, S., Edwards, L. M. & Marques, S. C. (eds.) (2016). *The Oxford Handbook of Positive Psychology*. Oxford: Oxford University Press.
7 See www.viacharacter.org.
8 Ehrenreich, B. (2010). *Smile or Die: How Positive Thinking Fooled America and the World*. London: Granta.
9 Willig, R. (2013). *Kritikkens U-Vending – en Diagnose af Forvandlingen fra Samfundskritik til Selvkritik*. Copenhagen: Hans Reitzels Forlag.
10 See Urban Dictionary: www.urbandictionary.com/define.php?term=jomos [retrieved 19 Feb. 2018].

Value-ethical positions

The search for values as key drivers of human existence and behaviour can be traced back to classical Greek philosophy, to Plato, Socrates and Aristotle. In his book *Nichomachean Ethics* Aristotle proposes *eudaimonia* – Greek for well-being or happiness, often translated as doing well and living well – as the highest human aim. Coupled with *epieikeia* – another core principle, defined as equity based on a flexible situational assessment[11] – *eudaimonia* can offer an important guideline and serve as the highest aim of human thinking and acting in practice. Aristotle's position can be described as *situational ethics*. *Eudaimonia* frames our eternal quest for a just and decent life, which requires continuous ethical reflections. Aristotle describes the path to *eudaimonia* as being based on *good character and education/culture* (*ētos* in Greek – pronounced with a long 'e'), which is achieved by striving for *good habits* (*étos* in Greek – pronounced with a short 'e'). Aristotle underscores that character can be developed in cooperation with a teacher (for example a good dialogue guide) and through deliberate and carefully considered choices. This path is defined by ethical decisions based on independence and agency – not external advantages. Aristotle emphasizes that *eudaimonia* should always be chosen independently and never out of concern for anything else (for example honour, joy, reason, duty and virtues),[12] with altruism and selflessness guiding our choices. From this perspective, striving for *eudaimonia* should be the overriding aim. Values may be viewed as inherent, meaning that the individual prefers what is good, guided by his or her character and education/culture. According to Aristotle, inherent values – possibly both good and bad – provide a clear orientation where ethical decisions are, ideally, guided by *courage* and *generosity*. Any act is a manifestation of the individual's virtues, and virtues are good when they are present in a fully flourishing person. Aristotelian ethics are dominated by the ontological assumption that human beings will strive for what is good.[13]

During the Age of Enlightenment, the German philosopher Immanuel Kant, in particular, was critical of this focus on happiness and well-being. Kant advocated an ethic where the individual citizen or ruler is driven by a *duty* to do what is best for the community. In his principal treatise from 1781, *Critique of Pure Reason*,[14] Kant proposes a c*ategorical imperative*: *Act only in accordance with that maxim*

---

11 Vega, J. (2013). Legal rules and epieikeia in Aristotle: Post-positivism rediscovered. In L. Huppes-Cluysenaer and N. M. M. S. Coelho (eds.), *Aristotle and the Philosophy of Law: Theory, Practice and Justice. Ius Gentium: Comparative Perspectives on Law and Justice* 23, pp. 171–200. Dordrecht: Springer Science+Business Media.

12 Cf. Aristotle (1999). *Nicomachean Ethics* (translated by W. D. Ross). Book 1, 7; p. 10. Kitchener: Batoche Books. http://socserv.socsci.mcmaster.ca/~econ/ugcm/3ll3/aristotle/Ethics.pdf [retrieved 21 Jan. 2016].

13 Ontology deals with human beings' physical and mental well-being and what determines the individual.

14 Kant, I. (1998). *Critique of Pure Reason*. Cambridge, UK: Cambridge University Press (Original German edition 1781).

through which you can at the same time will that it become a universal law. Here, the ethics of duty determines value-based human decisions.

The third ethical position, so-called *consequentialism* or *utilitarianism,* differs from both Aristotle's situational ethics and Kantian duty ethics. In consequentialism, norms and values depend on the *consequence* or *utility* of an act for the community and society. In this sense, consequences are the touchstone for whether a given act is morally right or wrong.

Although ethical considerations in connection with individual decision-making will often be driven by several, overlapping ethical principles, I adopt the following position: in light of the contemporary trends in society outlined above, with growing individual self-control, self-monitoring and self-improvement craze, it would not always seem appropriate to subject oneself to Kant's *duty ethics,* where one's ethical position is detached from one's situational judgement and is guided only by what is *required.*[15] Further, it is not always appropriate to base one's choice on a consideration of the *consequences,* since such an assessment may determine whether one finds that one has the necessary resources, time or energy to act. Thus, in some situations, consequentialism or utilitarianism may place an undue constraint on the individual's consideration of more complex situational factors. It is important to be able to opt out, even if it may be both more utilitarian and more ethically honourable to act.

Aristotle's ontological and *situationally ethical position* is a useful approach in coaching and other professional dialogues, and it can in fact be seen to play a role in certain current coaching approaches. This ethical position constitutes one of the pillars of the value-oriented dialogue approaches described in the present book. One example of this in the international literature is *coaching with compassion,* a concept that was developed by the organizational scholar Boyatzis and colleagues.[16] Unlike coaching that is focused on deficiencies and compliance, coaching with compassion concerns itself more with the needs of the coachee. Based on the coach's empathy with the dialogue partner, compassionate coaching seeks to enable learning and development with the ultimate aim of improving the coachee's well-being. A similar orientation that strengthens the individual's agency through empathy and compassion is also pursued in third-generation coaching and in protreptic or value-ethical conversations.

Value – an attempt at a definition

In the following, I make an attempt to define *value* as an important landmark for coaching and other developmental dialogues. 'Value' is a broad term with many

---

15 Duty ethic is a deontological ethic, that is, it is not determined by the person but by what is required – without a direct focus on the consequences. The crux is whether the action is morally appropriate.
16 Boyatzis, R. E., Smith, M. L. & Beveridge, A. J. (2013). Coaching with compassion: Inspiring health, well-being and development in organizations. *Journal of Applied Behavioral Science,* 49, 2, 153–178.

meanings, but they all imply some sort of influence on our behaviour. Based on others' research, Schwartz proposes the following definition: values are criteria that we use to select and justify actions and to evaluate people (including ourselves) and events.[17] Below, I list the six value categories included in Schwartz's[18] value theory (written in italics) along with my own, added comments:

1 *Values are beliefs* linked inextricably to affect. When values are activated, individuals react emotionally – with joy, apprehension or anger – depending on the situation and the behaviour of possible others.
2 *Values refer to desirable goals.* As described earlier (Figure 4.1 in Chapter 4) value orientation is positioned at the top of the intentionality hierarchy. Goals can be adapted more readily. Values are fundamental for the individual's action orientation.
3 *Values transcend specific actions and situations.* Thus, values have a more fundamental meaning to people. This implies that values are more fundamental than norms and attitudes, which are more closely associated with specific situations and contexts.
4 *Values serve as standards or criteria* that guide our evaluation of actions, policies, people and events. We evaluate these as being good or bad, fair or unfair, often by predicting benefits or consequences. Often, we are not aware of the influence of values but they come up in dilemma situations, where certain values clash.
5 *Values are ordered by importance.* Some values have near-universal status, while others are culturally, individually or contextually determined. Universal values can be described using the Greek matrix with four core values: goodness, truth, equity and beauty, with *phrónesis*, value-based agency, at the centre.[19] Values are ranked by the importance they hold for the individual and the importance they hold in the given context.
6 The relative *importance of multiple values guides action*. This prioritization thus also describes how values may differ between individuals and, often, between different stages in life. Values are a fundamental driver of individual behaviour, and hierarchically, values are placed above norms and attitudes.

Values are a key anchor for our identity, and they link our actions to our ethical beliefs. A value implies a capacity to act and often reflects our implicit desire to act in a way that is aligned with our experience, knowledge and ethical beliefs. When our actions are aligned with our values, we act with certainty,

---

17 Schwartz, S. H. (1992). Universals in the content and structure of values: Theoretical advances and empirical tests in twenty countries. *Advances in Experimental Social Psychology*. San Diego: Academic Press, vol. 25, 1.
18 Schwartz, S. H. (2012). *An Overview of the Schwartz Theory of Basic Values*. Online Readings in *Psychology and Culture*, 2(1). http://dx.doi.org/10.9707/2307-0919.1116.
19 See Kirkeby, O. F. (2016). *Protreptik – Selvindsigt og Samtalepraksis*. Frederiksberg: Samfundslitteratur, p. 196. See also: Kirkeby, O. F. (2009). *The New Protreptic*. Copenhagen: CBS Press.

resolution and commitment. From his phenomenological position Kirkeby describes value as an *I can*.[20] This sense of agency – a sense of being one's own master – stems from our knowledge, previous experiences and anticipations and is also influenced and guided by an ethical evaluation that may be both reflective and intuitive.[21]

Reflections on values, which inform our individual interactions with our environment and ultimately shape the specific purposes and goals of our actions, thus play a crucial role in generating transformative and fruitful dialogues. Speaking about core concepts and values helps individuals, teams or departments develop the capacity to act with conviction, attitude and agency in the situation. Thus, our values provide our actions with ethically founded legitimacy and serve as landmarks that help us navigate with implicit certainty in specific, potentially challenging situations. Describing values as implicit means that they are always present as an integral part of our capacity to act and as a basis of our determination and motivation to act in the world. Values *inhabit us*, as Kirkeby[22] puts it.

Conscious reflection, including ethical reflection, can be unfolded in a coaching conversation and in other types of transformative and fruitful dialogues. For example, the dialogue partner is invited to explore an important event in depth, or the conversation may take its starting point in a particular theme or value that it then goes on to explore. In our everyday lives, many value judgements are pre-reflective (that is, they are not articulated or reflected upon), expressed through our intuitive way of acting in the situation. We have a sense in and of the event or the situation and act based on previous experiences, a *phronetic* capacity or event-sense. *Phrónesis* is an important concept in Greek philosophy. Aristotle thus defines five forms of knowledge: 1) *epistéme*, logical, rational, scientific and 'true' knowledge; 2) *technē*, skills-based knowledge; 3) nous, intellectual knowledge that develops with experience; 4) sophia, wisdom; and 5) *phrónesis*, often translated as practical or normative wisdom, a description that only partially captures the complexity of the concept. Aristotle describes *phrónesis* as virtue and 'a reasoned and true state of capacity to act with regard to the things that are good or bad for man'.[23]

Phrónesis is based on a specific attitude; an attitude that is founded in virtues and, ultimately, in specific values. Kirkeby also makes frequent use of the concept of *phrónesis* in a tradition that spans from Socrates and Plato to Aristotle:

20 Kirkeby, O. F. (2009). *The New Protreptic*. Copenhagen: CBS Press, p. 156.
21 With certain parallels, Bandura speaks of *perceived self-efficacy*; the theory is not, however, particularly rooted in phenomenology or value ethics but may be understood as a social learning theory or a social-cognitive theory. See Bandura, A. (2012). On the functional properties of perceived self-efficacy revisited. *Journal of Management*, 38(1), 9–44.
22 Kirkeby, O. F. (2016). *Protreptik – Selvindsigt og Samtalepraksis*. Frederiksberg: Samfundslitteratur, p. 169.
23 Aristotle (1999). *Nicomachean Ethics* (translated by W. D. Ross). Book 6: 'A reasoned and true state of capacity to act with regard to human good' (p. 95). http://socserv.socsci.mcmaster.ca/~econ/ugcm/3ll3/aristotle/Ethics.pdf [retrieved 21 June 2016).

phrónesis requires 'a perception of the good that is so fundamental, profound and binding that it inevitably leads to a spontaneous, practical application of valid, normative knowledge to the given situation'.[24] In this sense, *phrónesis* is a form of event-sense, agency or wisdom that is capable of translating values into action for the sake of what is good and right.

Values – universal or shaped in the dialogue

When values are introduced as a key indicator of reflections in the dialogue practice, it is important to specify how they are both individually determined and the result of a co-creative process between the dialogue participants. This calls for an epistemological clarification: are values inherent, or are they cul-tural and social phenomena? To some degree, both aspects apply. When we assume *eudaimonia* to be the highest human achievement and the highest aim of human striving and actions, the balance between individual values and societal ideals becomes crucial. This quest for *eudaimonia* requires the individual to reflect on core values that pave the way for ethical ways of acting in specific situations.

If we consider specific social settings and human interactions, values may appear as diverse, depending on context, culture and history. Social-constructionists tend to view values as a co-creative and collaborative outcome that takes shape within human relationships. In the social arena we have to explain and ultimately negotiate how our actions in specific contexts are based on and shaped by certain values. Social-constructionists recognize multiple perspectives in their efforts to prevent certain individual perspectives from dominating, suppressing or silencing others' perspectives. From this point of view it is important to dig a little deeper in order to try to understand how certain values, beliefs, aspirations, dreams and hopes can form the basis of actions by a given person or group. From a social-constructionist perspective it is important to maintain that everything meaningful in life – knowledge, thinking, behaviour – has its origin in the relations the individual is a part of. Viewed from this epistemological position values are not absolute; they are an outcome of a negotiation and dialogue process among the participants in groups, teams, organizations and society at large. However, I rely on the understanding that social-constructionists also assume that human beings strive for what is good. As Gergen puts it: 'At least one central ingredient [of the relationship] is the co-creation of a real and valued world'.[25] Striking a balance between the individual's inherent and practice-driven core values and the relationally created ethical foundation is one of the most important tasks in coaching and other professional and personal everyday conversations. Coaches and other dialogue guides should help the dialogue partner

---

24 Kirkeby, O. F. *et al.* (2008). *Protreptik – Filosofisk Coaching i Ledelse*. Frederiksberg: Samfundslitteratur, p. 90.
25 Gergen, K. J. (2010). *Relational Being. Beyond Self and Community*. Oxford: Oxford University Press, p. 174.

become aware of his or her core personal values and how these value positions are shaped in practice communities in personal and professional contexts.

Values as the ethical and action-oriented basis of the dialogue

Value-oriented dialogues and third-generation coaching can strengthen an individual's ethically founded agency. It is therefore important to move away from the narrow focus on goals and achievements that characterizes simple coaching techniques, which ultimately confine the person to the regimen of self-control and self-monitoring (see Chapter 2). The individual's ethical base should neither have duty nor potential consequences as its dominant concern. Instead, the individual's or the group's embeddedness in a specific context and situation should form the basis of possible ethical reflections, where *striving for what is good* serves as the ethical maxim for both the individual and the community. However, general, abstract and anonymous reflections on key concepts and values can also form the basis of an ethical clarification that prepares the individual person to handle a specific situation. This general approach may for example be driven by the question, 'What does *agency* mean to you?' This will be addressed in more detail in the next section.

Any dialogue is a journey that enhances the individual's *character and education/culture* (*ētos* in Greek, with a long 'e') and helps build *good habits* (*étos* in Greek, with a short 'e'). Reflecting on values takes the dialogue participants on a Grand Tour, existentially speaking. Professional and personal everyday dialogues and third-generation coaching can form settings for practicing self-care and compassion with others. They can support the development of good judgement, thus expanding both the individual's and the community's capacity to act based on ethical and value-based reflections. This ethical judgement is not always straightforward. Situational ethical reflections enable us to examine dilemmas, where different values and ethical positions clash and maybe contradict each other. In the dialogue, the dilemma should be considered a valuable occasion for further reflection. The dialogue participants immerse themselves in a slow and careful search for ethical clarity – without feeling pressured into a limp compromise. It is through this process that the dialogue participants develop *ētos*.

Unlike externally imposed rules and simplistic instructions and guidelines, values reflect our ethical foundation and thus what the individual perceives as meaningful in his or her actions. Values reflect our professional and personal identity. In a management context the leader's value-based actions are mediated by virtues, which Kirkeby describes as follows:[26]

---

26 Kirkeby, O. F. (2000). *Management Philosophy: A Radical-Normative Perspective*. Berlin/Heidelberg/New York: Springer.

1   *eubolia*: careful deliberation; ability to see things in a new light; ability to see possibilities;
2   *euphoria*: unambiguous commitment; a sense of reality; ability to lead;
3   *hypomoné*: capacity for patience, self-restraint, allowing events to unfold;
4   *prolépsis*: imagination, anticipation;
5   *maieutics*: literally 'midwifery', letting the people one leads seek motivations for what they do;
6   *epibolé*: intuition based on bodily experience.

Working with values in coaching and other fruitful dialogues

Essentially, I see two possible ways of incorporating reflections on values in the dialogue process. One is a dialogue form or coaching conversation that applies a purely protreptic perspective, operating exclusively on an abstract and anonymous level and avoiding actual events and narratives as key elements in the conversation. The other is a dialogue form or coaching conversation that includes the individual's or group's *real-life contexts* and only incorporate value reflections at a later stage. Both approaches strive for a *critical, existential intensity*.[27]

What is the basic structure of the two dialogue approaches?

1   *The protreptic approach:* Here, the dialogue takes its point of departure in a specific value or concept (such as courage, agency, responsibility, sincerity, decency). The conversation is abstract and anonymous, that is, detached from specific events and from any narratives related to specific situations or events. This *ētos*-building journey begins with a focus on a core value or important concept; it is a journey that is initiated by the dialogue guide or protreptician, but which ultimately – due to its abstract nature – becomes a journey of discovery for both participants. A deliberate reflection on a certain concept or value can help us reach (some degree of) clarity on who we are, who we would like to be, or how things are or can become meaningful for us (the dotted arrow in Figure 4.1). Within a protreptic framework, the dialogue participants choose a path that leads, more or less directly, to a clarification of values. Through this reflective process, the individual (or the group, team or department) develops a capacity for acting with certainty and inner strength in future situations. In protreptic the individual is oriented towards what is *the most essential in his or her life*, the fundamental ethical beliefs and values that gradually take shape during this type of conversation. *Protreptikos* was originally developed by Aristotle as an invitation to the ruler to grapple with philosophy.[28] Kirkeby can be credited

---

27 Kirkeby, O. F. (2016). *Protreptik – Selvindsigt og Samtalepraksis*. Frederiksberg: Samfundslitteratur, p. 367.
28 See the reconstruction and German translation by G. Schneeweiß: Aristoteles (2005). *Protreptikos – Hinführung zur Philosophie*. Darmstadt: Wissenschaftliche Buchgemeinschaft. Or the English-

for bringing this dialogue form into the current age.[29] It can be compared to Socrates's so-called '*maieutics*', 'midwifery', which Kierkegaard also draws on.[30] Kirkeby has enriched classical protreptic with an etymological dimension, driven by the notion that words serve as sensuous landmarks that combine sensations, imagery, emotions and thinking by branching out into related words and thus generating the mental network that makes thinking possible. Words also allow us to articulate value-related feelings and thus translate them into reflection horizons and critical-affirmative evaluation mechanisms for our own practice. Moreover, words are vessels of social history, particularly the history of power. For historical reasons, Aristotle does not include this linguistic perspective in his version of protreptic. With its exclusive focus on values and core concepts and their interrelatedness and kinship, protreptic casts the dialogue participant as a *human being* rather than a person with certain roles, embedded in a given context. Protreptic can help us clarify values as a basis for experiencing ourselves as masters of our own lives, that is, for developing an implicit, almost bodily rooted capacity to act in the way that feels right and good.

2   *The situational approach*: During the conversation the dialogue partner describes a specific situation, event or task, often one that constitutes a challenge. Jenny Rogers[31] describes this process as a way to 'walk through an issue instead of just talking about it'. In cooperation with the dialogue guide or coach, the dialogue partner can examine the situation more closely, see his or her habits in a new light, put his or her implicit behaviour in the situation into words by reflecting on and reliving details and thus gradually get in touch with key issues, motives, attitudes, beliefs, values and aspirations. By focusing on the specifics, the dialogue guide or coach gets to know the other's life world better, which in turn lays a foundation for a co-creative dialogue that makes it possible to deconstruct the narrative about certain situation and events. Reliving and reflecting on behaviour can *provide a basis for discussing core concepts or values* that the dialogue guide comes to see as essential to the dialogue partner, or which the dialogue partner keeps returning to and wishes to examine more closely. When the dialogue guide has heard the dialogue partner's story, the guide can use the narrative as an entrance point, for example by asking, 'How would you name the story you

language reconstruction, which can be downloaded from www.protrepticus.info/protr2017x20.pdf [retrieved 19 Feb. 2018].
29 The most recent publication is Kirkeby, O. F. (2016). *Protreptik – Selvindsigt og Samtalepraksis.* Frederiksberg: Samfundslitteratur.
30 See Søltoft, P. (2008). Kierkegaard som coach. *Erhvervspsykologi*, 6, 1, 2–17. See also Søltoft, P. (2015). *Kunsten at Vælge Sig Selv – Om Kierkegaard, Coaching og Lederskab.* Copenhagen: Akademisk Forlag.
31 Rogers, J. (2012). *Coaching Skills*. Berkshire: Open University Press, p. 190: 'walk through an issue instead of just talking about it'.

just told me? What title do you want to give it?' The dialogue partner may say, for example, 'It's a story about *courage*!' Through the subsequent, more abstract reflection on concepts or values, the dialogue partner comes into close contact with his or her own identity landscape and self-concept. Ultimately, it will also be possible to engage in a protreptic conversation about courage. In this way, the reflection on values can help lay a good, new foundation for acting. Towards the end, the conversation may then return to a specific real-life situation or context, which the person will now be able to handle with greater certainty whenever it comes up again. The situational approach makes it possible to take the dialogue partner's specific contextual challenges seriously while also taking the conversation to a higher level, where the dialogue partner can clarify his or her values in a more general sense and thus develop a greater capacity to act in the future.

In the case story below I describe how a dialogue that initially revolves around a specific situation moves to the more abstract level of protreptic reflection.

Coaching with Eve

Eve, who is 30 years old, had had several conversations with me in my capacity as her mentor. She has an academic degree and is an ambitious project manager at a university; her job involves major responsibilities and good career development opportunities. Eve told me about the expectations that her colleagues and, particularly, her supervisor had of her. She found it difficult to navigate in a set-up where there were no 'natural' boundaries between her work and personal life. Her situation was particularly challenging, because her mobile phone was paid for by her employer. During her conversations with me she insisted that she kept the phone turned off after work, and that she was very reluctant to work outside her normal office hours. 'Spending time with my friends is my top priority – I need time off, and I also love dancing. My free time is hugely important to me,' she said. Together, Eve and I examined her dilemma: what was the real issue for her with the expectations from her supervisor and colleagues, and how important was her free time to her? We explored her feelings and commitment at work, her satisfaction when she made a difference, and when she was able to achieve development and success in the various projects she was involved in. We also looked at her experiences during her time off, her desire to dance and spend time with others, including her friends. How did Eve seek and find meaning in her life? At one point, as we were reaching an understanding of her dilemma, I asked Eve what *freedom* meant to her. At first, she was taken aback by my question, but when I described the potential utility of examining a concept that I considered to be very essential to her life, she was very interested in exploring this word with me. The abstract reflection, where I can contribute, as a fellow human being, took our conversations to a new level. Our reflections on what we heard when we spoke about freedom[32] added new quality to our understanding of her dilemma. This reflection on the concept of *freedom* ultimately helped Eve realize that she should never compromise on her passion to co-create something with others, whether it was in dance or in certain processes at work.

Closing remarks

The purpose of this chapter has been to underscore the role that values play in coaching and other fruitful professional and private everyday dialogues. It was illustrated that values are fundamental to our identity and to our striving for ethically founded ways of acting. Values establish a degree of certainty in an individual or in a group of people with regard to why and how they wish to act. From this perspective, values can be viewed as essential for bringing substance to the conversation. It should be underscored, however, that a focus on values, important concepts or key themes is not necessarily associated with any specific kind of coaching or dialogue practice, but as a dialogue guide one can always include reflections on values in the conversation. To achieve this ambition it is crucial to explain the utility of reflecting on values to the dialogue partner. It is important to introduce the topic and to clarify the contract. The concept, topic or value must be explicitly put on the agenda. It does not come up on its own, without an explicit effort. Hence, it is important at the beginning of the dialogue to establish one's role as the dialogue guide, who takes responsibility for setting the stage in a way that provides a calm space for reflection and contemplation.

---

32 Kirkeby (2015) speaks of translocutionarity, a term he phrased, which describes the phenomenon that one only understands one's own thoughts when they are said aloud.

Chapter 6

The narrative perspective
Transformation through sharing

Throughout history, people have told each other stories as a way to share important events, sorrows and joys. Narratives or stories have helped shape cultures, transform them, and pass traditions on to future generations. For the individual, narratives lay the foundation for creating and shaping oneself and for developing one's identity and self-understanding. In our hypercomplex world, where grand narratives have lost their power of identification or legitimation, the power of narratives can take on new meaning. Personal experiences and reflections enable a person to become an active co-narrator in the dialogue, thus contributing and acting as a supportive partner to someone who wants to be able to handle his or her life situation and particular challenges in a new and more adaptive way.

In this chapter I examine the role of the narrative for the way we speak to each other. Narratives help make meaning for an individual, while for a community they help establish a collective understanding. We develop through dialogue – individually, in groups and in organizations. Narratives are bearers of inherent values. Through the narrative we can express things that are important to us. In the following, the narrative understanding rests on an epistemological theory, which combines the phenomenological-existential and social-constructionist epistemology into a new whole. As part of our dialogue practice, narratives and the narrative co-creative approach lays a foundation that integrates the basic themes presented in previous chapters – meaning and values – into a single whole.

Stories – narration – a definition

Etymologically, 'narration' stems from two different Latin terms: *narrare* (to tell, relate, recount) and *gnarus* (to know, the root of 'knowledge'[1]). Thus, the word narration has two dimensions. Through storytelling, individuals connect with others, inviting them into their life, also by explaining themselves and their own previous and potential future actions. With the story as a vehicle, the storyteller

---

1 See Online Etymology Dictionary: Narration, www.etymonline.com [accessed 29 Feb. 2016].

also tries to convey a *truth*. Many of the stories we hear, even if we are aware that some of them may have to be taken with a grain of salt. Thus, any narrative exists somewhere on a scale between truth and fiction. This brings a dynamic element to the story. It develops independently of the context, the listener or the dialogue partner and of the storyteller's own understanding and state of mind.

A narrative can be defined[2] as

> an account that ties events together to form a pattern and a timeline with the purpose of producing a plot and an action-driven logic. The narrative ties past, present and future together and is thus both retrospective and directed at the future. The narrative always contains a performative element that underscores and explains the narrator's self-concept and identity-related ambitions.

Based on this definition, the self emerges as a result of the person's narrative efforts to shape him/herself in a particular way. In this narrative understanding, the person's perceived identity cannot be viewed as a stable entity but as the result of a continuous striving to tell him/herself and others who he or she is. While acknowledging that certain features of the self are present from birth, Bruner describes his understanding of the self as follows: 'there is no such thing as an intuitively obvious and essential self to know, one that just sits there ready to be portrayed in words. Rather, we constantly construct and reconstruct our selves to meet the needs of the situations we encounter, and we do so with the guidance of our memories of the past and our hopes and fears for the future'.[3] To the existential philosopher Søren Kierkegaard, the self is *a task*, and the key is *how* we choose. *Choosing oneself* is a lifelong ethical requirement that involves a continually developing self-narrative.[4]

If the self can be regarded as a product of narratives that ultimately involve ethical reflections, it is obvious that professional conversations and other types of dialogues can play a crucial role in bringing out a new self-narrative and, thus, a new self-concept in the person seeking support. The dialogue guide asks questions about the person and his or her story, which can be expanded and modified by incorporating new events, interpretations, perspectives and certain ethical value reflections. This will be discussed in more detail in Part III.

---

2 See Bruner, J. (2002). *Making Stories: Law, Literature, Life*. New York, NY: Farrar, Straus and Giroux; Sarbin, T. R. (ed.) (1986). *Narrative Psychology: The Storied Nature of Human Conduct*. New York, NY: Praeger; Freeman, M. (2014). Narrative, ethics, and the development of identity. *Narrative Works: Issues, Investigations, & Interventions* 4(2), 8–27.
3 Bruner, 2002, p. 64.
4 See Kierkegaard, S. (1983). *The Sickness unto Death: A Christian Psychological Exposition for Upbuilding and Awakening (Kierkegaard's Writings*, Vol. 19). (H.V. Hong & E.H. Hong, Eds.). Princeton, New Jersey: Princeton University Press. See also: Stark, G. J. (1973). Kierkegaard: The self and ethical existence. *Ethics*, 83, 108–125.

Narratives shape meaning and reflect values

Narrative content highlights certain events because the right selection and plot sequences shape the story and the action logic into behaviour patterns that the narrator wishes to convey. The plot reveals an underlying *meaning*, brought out by the narrative. The connection between narrating and meaning-making can be viewed as a circular process. Storytelling brings out meaning, which is in turn elucidated and shaped through the storytelling, as the storyteller pursues a particular intention. A storyteller opens an important story with 'Listen . . .'. He or she seeks to convey a specific message, for example, 'I am stressed at work', 'I had an amazing holiday', 'The new challenges are putting me under a lot of pressure'. Simultaneously, meaning emerges during the telling. Meaning is created in the narrative flow, especially when the storyteller has an interested listener, who asks questions and empathizes with the other, as the narrative unfolds. Thus, the story reflects the individual's attempt at meaning-making in his or her life, and at the same time it is often a product of the dialogue community in which the story is being told. Particularly in fruitful professional everyday dialogues and coaching, the dialogue guide plays an important role in this co-creative process. The narratively oriented sociologist Arthur Frank speaks of *post-autonomy ethics* in the consultation.[5] A dialogue guide, counsellor or coach positions him/herself as a listener who meets the storyteller at eye-level with a calm and focused presence, a state that is also expressed bodily. Frank even says that sometimes the storyteller can even arrive at new insights simply by having an attentive listener.

Through storytelling, the storyteller also seeks to express and capture *what is existentially meaningful*. By carefully choosing and portraying certain select events, persons and situations the storyteller more or less explicitly presents *values* that play an important role in the storyteller's life, and which represent a certain character and meaning to him or her. Stories express and reflect the storyteller's implicit value base. Values are thus articulated through the story. Values that are captured in concepts such as 'courage', 'love', 'respect', 'decency' or 'agency' are highlighted and vitalized by being bound into a narrative. A story can exemplify and clarify, for example, what role 'courage' or 'agency' plays in a person's life. The story's plot and action logic highlight 'courage' or 'decisiveness' as a particularly important value for the storyteller. Or a story might lead to certain values or concepts being filtered out: while telling the story, the storyteller may, for example, come to realize how much courage or decisiveness she showed in a particular situation. Thus, storytelling also reflects the person's ethical orientation and positioning. The storyteller becomes aware of the important

---

5 Frank, A. W. (2014). Narrative ethics as dialogical storytelling. In *Narrative Ethics: The Role of Stories in Bioethics, Special Report, Hastings Center Report* 44, no. 1, 16–20. DOI: 10.1002/hast.263. Frank is best known for his book *The Wounded Storyteller* from 1995, where he reflects on the narrative with inspiration from his own experiences as a cancer patient.

role of courage and decisiveness in her life. Storytelling involves relating to oneself, to others, to the environment and, ultimately, to the listener.[6]

From a pre-arranged position, the dialogue guide can act as a supportive partner in the dialogue and thus encourage a focus on values. Within a narrative framework, the dialogue guide will be able to ask the storyteller, 'What name or title do you want to give your story?' This elevates the story to a value level. The storyteller might answer, 'It's a story about "courage" and "decisiveness"'. Once the title has been articulated, the dialogue guide can invite the storyteller to reflect further on *courage* and *decisiveness* in a more abstract sense (see also Chapter 5[7]). In this way, protreptic reflections can be interwoven with the narrative discourse. This example may serve to illustrate how the protreptic dialogue form and the narrative approach can be integrated in a fruitful and enriching manner. The general perspective implied in a protreptic reflection on values can grow out of the specific story. This takes the situation-specific aspects of the story to the level of general human reflection that is the essence of protreptic.[8] The name of the story (in this case 'courage' and 'agency') can also form the framework of an *externalization*, as the storyteller reflects on the question and thus learns to detach him/herself from the problem or challenge – viewing the problem or challenge from an external position or from a different vantage point.[9]

The basic assumptions of the narrative approach

The understanding of narrative thinking that is presented here is not exclusively based on the work of Michael White,[10] although he is a very influential voice with regard to narrative practice, including my own. Narrative theory is broadly anchored in the social sciences and in qualitative research, with a special focus on *understanding the subjects' life world*.[11] My effort to balance the phenomenological-existential and the social-constructionist traditions is driven by the following insight: it is essential for me to have a deeper understanding of the uniquely subjective in my interaction with others, but I also continue to draw inspiration from social-constructionist theory. It is important to point out that, in contrast to some psychodynamic or psychological personality theories, I do not

---

6 An interesting read on this topic is Paul Ricoeur (1992). *Oneself as Another*. Chicago: University of Chicago Press.
7 See the section 'Working with values as part of coaching and other fruitful dialogues' in Chapter 5.
8 Originally, Ole Fogh Kirkeby rejected the narrative approach as a relevant element in the protreptic approach. Recently he has shown greater receptiveness to it; see Kirkeby, O. F. (2016). *Protreptik – Selvindsigt og Samtalepraksis*. Frederiksberg: Samfundslitteratur (Chapter 26).
9 See more about externalization in the section 'Directing attention at the problem – not at the person's shortcomings' in Chapter 7. See also: White, M. (1995). *Re-Authoring Lives*. Adelaide: Dullwich Centre Publications.
10 For example, White, M. (2007). *Maps of Narrative Practice*. New York, NY: Norton.
11 Smith, B. & Sparkes, A. C. (2006). Narrative inquiry in psychology: Exploring the tensions within. *Qualitative Research in Psychology*, 3, 169–192.

view the subject as having an *essence* or a *core self*. To me, the subject is a dynamic being who is shaped through subjective experiences and in collaborative and relational processes that take place in the dialogue and in the person's interactions with others in the social environment. In the following, I therefore briefly revisit the three fundamental assumptions that I have presented earlier,[12] which outline my epistemological foundation for developing third-generation coaching and other professional and transformative dialogues:

1 *Agency* describes the human capacity to choose among different options, to make choices, to mobilize energy and to act deliberately on the basis of own considerations and plans. In this understanding, the individual is assigned a proactive relationship with the world: human beings are able to take initiatives and to take life in their own hands. Individuals can act on the basis of their own intentions, which are shaped by the individual's active interchanges with the social and material environment, and not only by external impulses or determined by 'fate'. When an individual speaks of his or her actions, the story takes its point of departure in certain events, which are linked together and structured into a plot that makes the story meaningful to the actor/story teller. Narrative thinking applies the metaphor of a *landscape of action*, a concept that was originally developed within literary theory and later transferred to psychology and narrative therapy.

2 *Intentionality* describes the actor's persistent orientation towards the environment, which is manifest in his or her intentions in relation to specific others, tasks or situations. In the act, the person always relates to the social and physical environment on a bodily and sensory level[13] and always has a reflective awareness of certain plans and purposes.[14] Generally, the person's intentionality is manifest in his or her values and meaningful actions. In dialogues, the dialogue partner's values are manifest, in part, in the aspirations and striving that he or she expresses when the conversation turns to certain (job) tasks or a potential future. As mentioned earlier, intentionality can be viewed as a three-tier hierarchy (cf. Figure 4.1), where the *goal* represents the most specific level, *purpose* marks the general perspective and *meaning* connects with personal values as the most overarching dimension of intentionality. In third-generation coaching and other fruitful and transformative dialogues the main focus will be on this top level, which pertains to the search for meaning and various value perspectives. Narrative practice uses the metaphor of the *landscape of identity*, which must always be viewed in relation to the *landscape of action* – the person's behaviour in certain specific

---

12 Stelter, 2012, pp. 126–127.
13 Here I refer to the one type of intentionality that is described in phenomenology. The body always has an intentional relatedness to the environment. We sense the world through our way of acting in it. See also Merleau-Ponty, 2012.
14 Here, intentionality is expressed through specific purposes and action plans.

contexts. Keeping the identity landscape metaphor in mind, the dialogue guide focuses on the dialogue partner's identity, that is, his or her thinking, feelings, beliefs and values. The concept of intentionality marks a theoretical perspective that is toned down in the social-constructionist literature.

3   *Deconstruction* refers to the possibility of change and of multiple possible interpretations; it originally emerged as a reaction to idealist philosophy and structuralist literature theory. Deconstructionists oppose the structuralist reductionist attempt at resolving inner narrative tensions in speech or writing. The deconstructionist perspective, by contrast, assumes that there are multiple possible interpretations and thus multiple realities hidden in the story. In fruitful dialogues the conversation partner seeks to reinterpret certain dominant and potentially troubling stories about specific realities and myths that might benefit from a reframing and an alternative narrative. According to White, deconstruction has to do with 'procedures that subvert taken-for-granted realities and practices'.[15] He wants to 'exoticise the familiar': by challenging our intimate relationship with certain ways of living and thinking and embarking on a journey of discovery in our own life, we can ultimately develop a new plot in potentially troubling narratives.

This triad forms an essential foundation for the dialogue guide's understanding of the dialogue partner. Ultimately, it reflects a certain view of what it means to be human and of the capacity of the dialogue to generate change and reorientation in specific contexts and interpersonal meetings.

Positions in the narrative situation

With inspiration from Rita Charon,[16] one of the founders of narrative medicine, I point to the three basic positions in the narrative situation – *attention*, *representation* and *affiliation* – which Charon employs in her narrative approach to patient care. My interpretation of these positions in relation to my own narrative-collaborative practice is as follows:

1   *Attention*: Attention is the key position for the dialogue guide. The attention is directed at the narrative: what am I hearing, in my role as a dialogue guide? Which words do I attribute special meaning? What does the narrator's voice sound like? What does my body tell me? What emotions are triggered in me? What captures my interest in particular? What do I notice? Are there any words that stand out? Do I notice any values that stand out in the story, which I can ask about? What should be included when I bring in written accounts

---

15 White, M. (1991). Deconstruction Therapy, *Dulwich Centre Newsletter*, 2.
16 Charon, R. (2006). *Narrative Medicine: Honoring the Stories of Illness.* New York, NY: Oxford University Press. And: Charon, R. (2005). Narrative Medicine: Attention, Representation, Affiliation. *Narrative, 13*(3), 261-270. Retrieved from http://www.jstor.org/stable/2007965

(my own and the dialogue partner's), and how does the author convey the most meaningful aspects?
2   *Representation*: How do I convey my impressions to my dialogue partner, verbally and perhaps in writing, where I attempt to capture those impressions that are meaningful to me? How can I share any written texts with the other (for example through so-called witnessing documents after the conversation)? How am I moved by the other? How do I present what stood out to me – with the utmost respect for the other?
3   *Affiliation*: Narrative work – in both speech and writing – reflect a connectedness and an attachment between the dialogue guide and the dialogue partner or within a dialogue group. Narrative dialogues and approaches are always characterized by a mutual relationship and by an abandonment of the individualist autonomy mindset, as both (all) parties move towards an affiliation that leads to a shared practice. This affiliation should ideally lead to a *sense of attachment* in both (all) parties. This sense of attachment can inspire trust and a sense of security in the dialogue partner, who may dare to open up and disclose more about him/herself. The affiliation lays the foundation for empathy that was previously highlighted as a characteristic of third-generation coaching.

The narrative as an element in co-creative dialogues

Storytelling is an important part of many dialogues. In transformative dialogues, the dialogue partner has an ambition of gaining more insight into the context and the events that the story seeks to capture. Transformative dialogues or coaching presuppose a desire to *remedy* something, remove the stone in the shoe or learn about something that is important in one's life. *Myths* are stories that should be challenged. Myths originally served the purpose of providing a sense of security and continuity in a self-narrative. We have certain stable stories about our loved ones, our colleagues, our working procedures and so forth, but at some point the myths stop being valid and need to be adjusted or replaced.[17] That can happen for a variety of reasons. Once a change process is initiated and pursued in the framework of a transformative, fruitful dialogue or coaching, the respective roles of the dialogue participants are clear: the dialogue partner seeks development, change and help. The dialogue guide offers help. The dialogue partner tells his or her story, and the dialogue guide's first task is to understand, empathize with and search for the plot, which is not necessarily evident to them both. The dialogue guide's questions can help clarify the plot, as the dialogue partner – through the dialogue guide's questions – gradually discovers what the 'issue' is. At this stage, the dialogue is about *searching for the plot*. Only once the plot or

---

17   See McAdams, D. P. (1993). *The Stories We Live By: Personal Myths and the Making of the Self.* New York, NY: The Guilford Press.

the narrative action logic has been revealed – sometimes more so to the dialogue guide than to the person who is seeking help – can the process of 'modifying' the story begin. There are many ways to bring change into the dialogue. In third-generation coaching the dialogue guide is a co-reflective and collaborative partner, an empathic and generous listener and a fellow human being in relation to the dialogue partner.

Closing remarks

One aspect of the art of lingering in dialogue is the co-creation of narratives. The dialogue partner tells a story that may turn out to be a myth, that is, a story that needs greater nuance and modifications because it confines the dialogue partner to a perceived identity that has come to feel too limiting. The dialogue guide's task is to empathize with the dialogue partner's life world – without becoming trapped in it. The dialogue guide challenges the narrative, because that is the nature of their mutual contract. A respectful way of challenging the dialogue partner is to include oneself and one's own experiences, reflections and sense of being moved by what one hears, understands and senses. This brings a shared humanity and real substance to the conversation, where both participants are moved and touched by the other. This mutual emotional engagement, humanity and symmetrical moments are generated in the dialogue.

This art of guiding dialogues – at times with moments of symmetry – is discussed in more detail in Chapter 8, which focuses especially on the quality of the relationship and the dialogue guide's ability to be a participant and a co-creator of alternative stories that can help the dialogue partner develop a new understanding of the world and of the challenges he or she is facing.

Part III

Reflections on dialogue practice

In this final part I wish to focus on practice. Naturally, it is difficult to *speak* about practice; it should be *practiced*, after all. Leading dialogues is an art, a way of being, a passion – and it should be practiced, lived and co-created in human interactions in real-life conversations. The dialogue guide – a coach, mentor, therapist, colleague or friend – is encouraged to relate to a fellow human being, who lives his or her life and who has his or her own thoughts, feelings and ways of acting and reacting. We are essentially strangers to one another, but we can be moved by another, empathize with another, without necessarily being swallowed up by the other's dilemmas, challenges, pain and sorrow. The art of being a supportive dialogue guide is to get involved and to show compassion and empathy without fusing with the other and his or her problems, challenges and life perspectives.

In this practice-oriented part of the book, my focus is not any specific method, unlike the many books on coaching that approach the dialogue from a variety of theoretical-methodological positions, such as psychodynamic, existentialist, systemic, cognitive, social-constructionist, narrative or other positions. Drawing on a number of theoretical positions, the following presentation takes its point of departure in the development of the dialogue guide's *relational competencies and virtues*. Whether and how the dialogue guide relates to the other is crucial for the successful and satisfactory course of transformative and fruitful dialogues. Psychotherapy and coaching research speaks of *common factors*. These are the factors that strengthen the coaching/therapeutic/dialogical relationship and alliance, and which most tried and tested approaches have in common, including cooperation and agreement about the approach, the development of a fruitful alliance, the dialogue guide's empathy, respect, appreciation, authenticity and sincere interest and a firm and clear footing in the chosen dialogue approach. Common factors are considered to have a crucial impact on the outcome of the conversation. Striking a balance between maintaining an explorative and curious 'distance' to the conversation partner on the one hand and being a fellow human being and showing attachment on the other should be a key ambition for the dialogue guide in order to bring intensity and movement into the conversation.

I now invite you, as my reader, to join me on a journey into a universe that it is difficult to learn about via a book, but which has to be practiced on the basis of your attitudes and ethical stance and the general theoretical-methodological understanding that I present in the following. The rest of the journey takes place in the real world of dialogues, training, supervision and reflective practice.[1]

---

1 See Chapter 6 in Stelter, R. (2014). *A Guide to Third Generation Coaching*. Dordrecht/Heidelberg/New York/London: Springer.

Chapter 7

Enhancing attention

Being attentive of oneself and one's dialogue partner is a crucial condition for achieving focused immersion in the dialogue. The participants in the dialogue should avoid striving for a specific solution or a quick fix. A conversation often begins with an examination of the situation, the context, the other or oneself and one's way of dealing with the situation. Enhanced attention helps us discover exactly where we are. We sense the tiny nuances that reveal themselves to our conscious mind, and we understand ourselves better. The dialogue guide should see it as his or her task to enhance the dialogue partner's attention – by noticing what is happening in the dialogue partner and in him/herself.

In this chapter, I examine certain specific ways of practising attention. Although they are derived from a variety of traditions, they are capable of supplementing each other in the dialogue practice. Striving for and enhancing attention is a central element of the art of lingering in dialogue. In describing his concept of 'eventuals', Ole Fogh Kirkeby points to prosoché, attention, as one of the key ways of being in a dialogue. He distinguishes between the following dimensions:

1 *Being attentive of oneself.*
2 *Being attentive of others.*
3 *Being attentive of what is happening.*
4 *Arousing attention.*
5 *Being attentive of one's attentiveness (meta-attentiveness).*

I describe perspectives of attention inspired by literature about attention from the fields of both psychology and dialogue philosophy. On the one hand, attention forms the basis for a certain way of being, while on the other hand, attention also contains a strategic-methodological perspective for the dialogue guide as an approach that helps create momentum in the conversation.

In the following, enhancing attention will be discussed from a variety of perspectives:

- *Enhancing attention to the implicit elements of the situation.*
- *Immersing oneself into the complexity of the situation.*
- *Adopting a wondering and appreciative stance.*
- *Enhancing attention to oneself and the other.*
- *Being attentive of the problem, not the other's shortcomings.*
- *Enhancing attention to the ethical value perspective.*

In closely examining and describing the individual method I identify the considerations for the way the dialogue is conducted, highlighting them in a box or a figure to help the reader distinguish between the overall methodological approach and the specific question technique and the guide's positioning.

The triangle of attention

Enhancing attention plays out in an interaction between three poles, as illustrated in Figure 7.1.

The figure illustrates the interrelatedness between the dialogue guide and the dialogue partner. Both focus on the theme of the dialogue, on themselves and on the way they relate to the theme and to each other. Within this co-creative attention space they find meaning and discover the underlying values as they emerge, unfolding them through their shared lingering and reflecting on the topic.

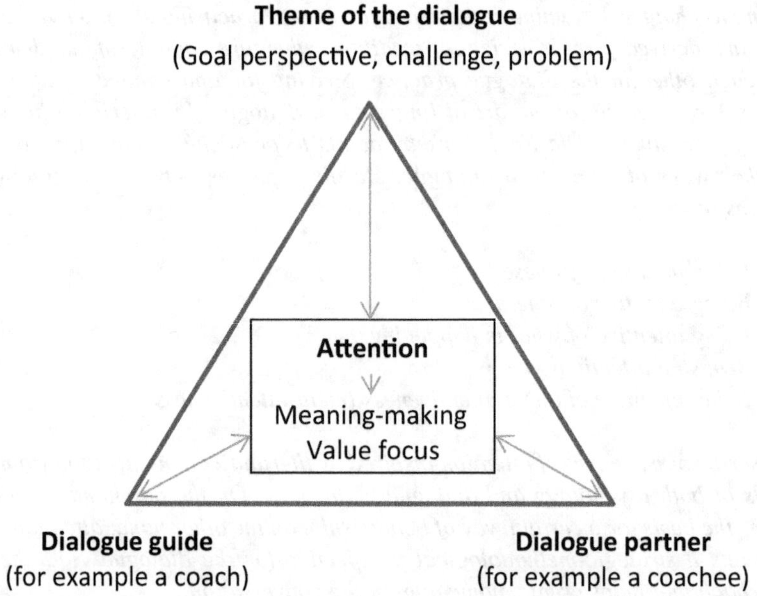

Theme of the dialogue
(Goal perspective, challenge, problem)

Attention
Meaning-making
Value focus

Dialogue guide
(for example a coach)

Dialogue partner
(for example a coachee)

Figure 7.1 The attention triangle: mutual influence and interaction between the dialogue participants about the subject of the dialogue.

Enhancing attention to the implicit aspects of the situation

Phenomenology focuses on subjective experiences, which are also the central topic in this section. Attention is directed at the individual's sensory experiences in the concrete *life world* that forms the topic of reflection and attention. Human actions, sensations, thoughts and feelings should always be considered in the specific, situated context. It is in the specific situation that meaning emerges and can be perceived. The body that senses its *relatedness* with the world plays an important role in everyday practice – although we are only partially aware of it when we act. Instead we rely on *tacit knowledge*. Tacit knowledge plays an important role in much of our everyday life. The body's tacit knowledge reflects a *practical consciousness*,[1] which is not reflected, and which the body has access to via prior experience. It is expressed through the person's actions in the practice field and through his or her habits and *habitus*.[2] It represents a pre-reflective, un-reflected state where one is not immediately able to describe one's behaviour in words. The problematic aspect of describing experiences is that we lack words to capture their full complexity. Language represents 'reality' in distinct units, word by word, and as such, is unsuited to conveying holistic phenomena. On the other hand, experiences are *perceived* as wholes, as singular, analogue phenomena. Hence, to the best of our ability, we need to find a way to put whole experiences into words. To get as close as possible to these holistic experiences, the dialogue guide may apply a *focusing* approach.[3]

> Sensory experiences are initially perceived as *a felt sense*, which stems from the immediate and felt meaning (felt sense) the person develops in a given situation, event or relationship with another person. Gendlin defines *felt sense* as follows:[4]
>
> > A felt sense is not a mental experience but a physical one. *Physical*. A bodily awareness of a situation or person or event. An internal aura that encompasses everything you feel and know about the given subject at a given time –
>
> *continued*

---

1 I use the concept here with reference to Giddens, A. (1984). *The Constitution of Society*. Cambridge: Polity Press, pp. 41ff.
2 The term *habitus* was introduced within the field of sociology by Norbert Elias (1969) and Pierre Bourdieu (1990). Elias defines habitus as our habits with regard to thinking, feeling and acting. Bourdieu expands this definition and regards *habitus* as a description of the person's particular social behaviour and acting, as conditioned by the person's social background and class-specific lifestyle.
3 Gendlin, E. T. (1982). *Focusing*. New York, NY: Bantam Books. Or Stelter, R. (2010). Experience-based, body-anchored qualitative research interviewing. *Qualitative Health Research*, 20(6), 859–867. See also www.focusing.org.
4 Gendlin, E. T. (1982). *Focusing*. New York, NY: Bantam Books, p. 37.

> encompasses it and communicates it to you all at once rather than detail by detail. Think of it as a taste, if you like, or a great musical chord that makes you feel a powerful impact, a big round unclear feeling.
>
> In the process of *focusing*, this *felt sense* is translated into metaphors and verbal imagery – the best way to capture experiential wholes from everyday practice. *Focusing* lets us use verbal images and metaphors to reframe pre-reflective sensory experiences and give them a verbal expression, even if we can never attain a one-to-one translation from sensations to language. Experiences will always be more complex than language can represent. Given the nature of language, imagery and metaphors offer the closest approximation to the actual sensory experience or impression. In this process we attach words and images to our sensations in a given situation which we then focus on in the dialogue. We linger in our sensations in order to grasp and immerse ourselves as fully as possible in the situation we put under the looking glass.

Immersion into the complexity of the situation

This immersion can be developed further via *the situation-specific perspective*, which I described in *A Guide to Third Generation Coaching*,[5] and which I will also bring into the present discussion. To encourage the person to immerse him/ herself in the complexity of the situation, the dialogue guide invites the person to examine his or her interaction with specific contexts. The guide can play an important role by supporting this examination. The situationally specific gaze enables the dialogue partner's immersion into his or her specific involvement in the context, which also forms the basis for a shared reflective focus between the dialogue participants (see Figure 7.2).

The situation-specific perspective helps establish a context that both dialogue participants can refer to. It is an indispensable condition for viewing the world from a *specific observer position*. Through the situationally specific gaze the dialogue participants bring depth to the many different aspects that any situation contains. The dialogue guide can help focus on the situational aspects and thus help the dialogue partner put into words what is often tacitly embedded in habits and routines. The dialogue guide's ability to ask the right questions is essential. These questions help to 1) bring depth to the perspective and thus form a basis for new insights and 2) enable new perspectives in relation to understanding and interpreting the specific situation.

---

5 Stelter, R. (2014). *A Guide to Third Generation Coaching*. Berlin: Springer, pp. 87–90.

Enhancing attention 85

Figure 7.2 Situation-specific perspective.

As a first step, the dialogue guide can *ask about a specific situation*, for example when the dialogue partner mentions stress or problems at work. The situation could be one in the recent past. The situation-specific perspective can also be used to examine a possible future or a desired situation that the dialogue partner is asked to envision. By directing attention to the selected situation the dialogue guide helps the partner exemplify and specify his or her experiences.

Next, the dialogue guide asks questions in a way that helps the dialogue partner *immerse him/herself in the situation* and uncover new facets through an in-depth description of the situation. This description may facilitate a deeper or new understanding of the situation. It also gives the dialogue guide a better understanding of the situation that makes it easier to *attune with* the dialogue partner's life world.

continued

> In the final phase, the dialogue guide aims deliberately to *foster a new orientation* by helping the dialogue partner move beyond the immediate everyday experience. Here, the participants examine the situation or the issue at hand from a wider perspective. This may be facilitated by circular questions (What does a good colleague have to say about the way you communicate?), by focusing on positive exceptions (Do you recall a situation where you found that you were able to communicate openly with someone?) or by focusing on the dialogue partner's strengths (Where does your strength lie in communicating with others? Are there certain situations where it has proved an advantage to communicate the way you do?).

The points in Figure 7.2 are intended as inspiration for examining the complexity of the situation from multiple angles. It is not intended as a complete model. The dialogue guide is invited to incorporate other and different perspectives than the ones included in the figure.

Adopting a wondering and appreciative stance

Lingering in the dialogue involves adopting a *wondering* stance in the I-thou relationship that forms the basis of a *genuine dialogue*. The dialogue philosopher Martin Buber describes the conversation as a profoundly existential process by using I-thou as key encounter: I and thou are each other's conditions, and as such they express the mutual relationship that is a prerequisite for lingering in the dialogue. The *I* comes into being in the relationship with the *thou*.[6] And in this mutual genesis, adopting a *wondering* stance towards the other *and* oneself is an important condition. Finn Thorbjørn Hansen describes this wondering as part of a good, philosophically oriented dialogue practice as follows:[7]

> Here, the philosophical practitioner and the guest meet, because they both have a vital and burning desire to become part of a larger community of wondering and conversation. Why? Because wondering and being deeply immersed in a conversation with another (or other) person(s) around a common cause ... for people can in itself feel profoundly rewarding, horizon-expanding and enjoyable. Even if the topics and the conversations may be painful, unsettling and provoking for both parties in the conversation.

---

6 See Buber, M. (1996). *I and Thou*. New York, NY: Touchstone (original from 1923).
7 Hansen, F. T. (2012). At være i en elskende relation med verden – hvorfor ikke al filosofisk praksis kan forveksles med terapi. *Norsk Filosofisk Tidsskrift, 47*(04), 270–276. See related publication: Hansen, F. T. (2016). Socratic wonder as a way to aletheia in qualitative research and action research. *HASER. Revista Internacional de Filosofía Aplicada*, 7, 51–88.

> The wondering perspective on the dialogue partner is based on one's own search for understanding. Both participants in the dialogue explore themselves and each other in an existentially exploratory manner. In wondering about the other, the dialogue guide essentially also looks for an answer that holds meaning for his or her own life. Although one has taken on the role as dialogue guide, one is going to encounter something in the other that is meaningful for one's own life world. It is in the wondering position that one meets the other as *a fellow human being*.

The *appreciative perspective* may be seen as a further step in a direction where the dialogue guide is not only a fellow human being but, with the other's consent, takes on a supportive role for another person, who is in doubt, seeking advice or hoping to turn his or her life around. At this point, the dialogue is not merely a human interchange, but a professional task with a strategic perspective. The appreciative approach is often misunderstood as a method that focuses exclusively on the positive. In its essence, it is *a way of examining and exploring* the dialogue partner's reality in a process of *appreciative inquiry*.[8] The approach has roots in both social-constructionist and narrative theory and also draws on aspects from positive psychology. The dialogue partner will often present a very one-sided view of the situation or event that is the topic of the conversation. From a deconstructionist perspective[9] the dialogue guide seeks to expand the dialogue partner's perception of and understanding for the situation by exploring aspects of the partner's experiential and perceptual universe that are not at the foreground of awareness, but which demand to be drawn out and recalled.

The case about Curt in the book *Third Generation Coaching* exemplifies the appreciative inquiry.[10] Curt has an executive position, and he comes to see me as a coach. He is very frustrated with his present job situation. In many regards, his worldview is very different from mine. That difference makes an empathic exploration particularly important and meaningful to me. I use my wondering to understand him as well as I can. I get the sense that *social interactions* with others are both a challenge and a dream for Curt. My view of Curt's life situation led me to the key, appreciative question of the whole process: 'Could you mention and describe a situation in your everyday life that you experience as meaningful, which you enjoy, and where you really appreciate social interactions with others?' And Curt immediately thinks of a situation: 'Yes, every year when I go to the

---

8 See Cooperrider, D. L., Whitney, D. & Stavros, J. M. (2008). *Appreciative Inquiry Handbook. For Leaders of Change*. (2nd edition). Brunswick, OH: Crown Custom Publishing.
9 See Chapter 6 in the present book, p. 76, note 3 (Deconstruction).
10 See Chapter 5.1.2. in Stelter (2014), *A Guide to Third Generation Coaching*. Berlin: Springer, pp. 147–152: 'Case 2: A little more Skanderborg in my life'.

Skanderborg Festival [a well-known Danish annual music festival] with some of my old friends'. In our continuing dialogue, this inclusion of a situation that had been outside Curt's awareness leads to a clear change in his view of social interactions – also in relation to his workplace – and eventually he changes his perception and his way of being in a way that makes him much happier with himself and with his life situation.[11]

> The core quality of appreciative inquiry is to look for situations where the dialogue participants perceive themselves to have strengths, resources and personal agency. These are often situations and events that have been forgotten, and which are now recalled via the dialogue guide's appreciative style, thus becoming part of the dialogue partner's conscious awareness as something valuable This recollection becomes the point of departure for shaping a new and more uplifting narrative, where the story's new plot (in Curt's case 'a little more "Skanderborg" in my working life') helps make a positive change or development process possible.

Enhancing attention to oneself and the other

These two attention perspectives interact, and they are, essentially, two sides of the same coin. Without attention to oneself, one cannot pay attention to the other. A professional dialogue guide in particular has to be aware of the contact boundaries that exist between him/herself and the other.

Attention to oneself

Attention to oneself is one of the fundamental stances that a competent dialogue guide must feel comfortable with. To coaches, psychotherapists, psychologists and other support persons, attention to oneself is a fundamental aspect of their professional ethics. There are many questions to reflect on: How does the dialogue partner's description affect me? What happens in me when I listen to the other? How am I drawn into the dialogue partner's narrative? What kind of pain, sorrow, compassion, joy, enthusiasm do I experience as a support person? What consequences does that empathy have on my way of relating to the dialogue partner, as he or she seeks support in dealing with a challenge or a difficult life situation? Am I, as a dialogue guide, becoming too engaged on the other's behalf? Am I seeking to realize my own ambitions or agenda through the other?

---

11 In Chapter 8, with the use of Figure 8.1, this case is further analysed from a narrative perspective.

Providing helpful support in a dialogue means striking a balance between engagement, empathy and understanding on the one hand and a certain detachment to the challenge on other. Otherwise one cannot maintain one's grasp of the bigger picture and a good contact with the dialogue partner. A key requirement for maintaining the professional position is to avoid *confluence* – a concept from gestalt practice that describes a mental state where two (or more) separate individuals have suspended the sense of any mutual distinction or boundary. However, other contact forms from gestalt theory are also relevant for the dialogue guide or professional to be aware of to prevent unfortunate consequences for fruitful interactions in the dialogue process:[12]

- *Introjection* refers to mental processes of uncritically and without further examination, judgement or differentiation internalizing perceptions, feelings and so forth in the meeting with the other.
- *Projection* refers to mental processes where some thoughts, perceptions, feelings and so forth that belong to oneself are attributed to the other. If these are negative elements that one would prefer to disown, projection may lead to anger, frustration and other negative feelings towards the other.
- *Deflection* refers to mental processes where one tries to avoid experiencing certain perceptions and feelings, for example by ignoring, distorting or laughing them off. However, deflection may also be a mental precondition for avoiding perceptions, thoughts and feelings that may be stressful to experience.
- *Retroflection* refers to mental processes where a certain mental and emotional energy that was originally directed at the outside world is held back within. Dysfunction within this contact domain may result in impulsive outbursts or excessive inhibition.

Good contact with oneself and the other occurs in 'healthy confluence'. This involves being fully present in the moment, being aware of oneself in the dialogue and in relation to the other and being aware of the boundaries between self and other. An important condition for this to happen is that one develops a sense of the other through a sense of oneself.

Attention to the other

Attention to the other is expressed via compassion, empathy and, ultimately, understanding the other's experiences, perceptions and interpretations of his or her world. Ole Fogh Kirkeby uses the philosophical dialogue concept of

---

12 Confluence and the other contact forms are described in Chapter 2 in Sonne, M. & Tønnesvang, J. (2015). *Integrative Gestalt Practice: Transforming Our Ways of Working With People*. London: Karnacology Publications.

heteroenticity – 'the ability to relate to oneself through the other'.[13] The dialogue guide generously makes him/herself available to the other with a basic stance of never knowing more than the other, that is, than the dialogue partner.

> From a psychological perspective attention requires a certain alertness from the dialogue guide. In the interaction with the dialogue partner the guide's attention to his or her own contact boundaries is particularly important. It is important to preserve one's integrity to avoid fusing – entering into confluence – with the other. Maintaining attention to the other along with an appropriate degree of detachment makes it possible to strike a good balance between *following and guiding*. The dialogue guide should pursue the other's best intentions by appreciating the dialogue partner's initiatives and recognizing him or her as a person with agency who is always seeking to find meaning in life. The dialogue guide also actively *guides* the dialogue partner, without, however, getting ahead of what the partner is ready and able to do. The dialogue guide should take charge of the process by actively leading the dialogue partner towards something.

The optimally supportive dialogue situation (for example in professional dialogues, coaching conversations and psychotherapy) can be described as an active cooperation between the dialogue guide and the dialogue partner, where *following and guiding are integrated into a creative dynamic*. The key is for the dialogue guide to maintain a constant focus on the dialogue partner's or client's conditions and experiences by presenting suggestions and questions as options rather than expert statements or statements of truth.[14]

An important topic in relation to attention to the other is *empathy*, which is one of the key basic positions the dialogue guide should adopt in conversations with the dialogue partner. Carl Rogers is an important voice in defining empathy, which he describes as the therapist's or, here, the dialogue guide's 'sensitive ability and willingness to understand the client's thoughts, feelings and struggles from the client's point of view. . . . [the] ability to see completely through the

---

13 A neologism in Kirkeby, O. F., Hede, T. D., Mejlhede, M. & Larsen, J. (2008). *Protreptik – Filosofisk Coaching i Ledelse*. Frederiksberg: Samfundslitteratur, p. 133.
14 These considerations are described in a larger context in a chapter on an emotion-focused approach in Stelter (2012) pp. 139–143. More of this approach in Greenberg, L. (2002). *Emotion-Focused Therapy: Coaching Clients to Work Through Feelings*. Washington, DC: American Psychological Association Press. Or, more briefly, in Elliott, R., & Greenberg, L. (2007). The essence of process-experiential/emotion-focused therapy. *American Journal of Psychotherapy*, 61(3), 241–254. From a philosophical dialogue perspective the reader can also find inspiration in Kirkeby, O. F. (2016). *Protreptik – Selvindsigt og Samtalepraksis*. Frederiksberg: Samfundslitteratur (Chapter 30: Måden at spørge).
15 As quoted in Kirk J. Schneider, J. Fraser Pierson & James F. T. Bugental (eds.) (2014). *The Handbook of Humanistic Psychology: Theory, Research, and Practice*. London: Sage Publications.

client's eyes, to adopt his frame of reference'.[15] Elsewhere in the same volume he adds, 'It means entering into the private perceptual world of the other ... being sensitive, moment by moment, to the changing felt meanings which flow in this other person ... it means sensing meanings of which he or she is scarcely aware'.[16] It is this ultimate attention to the other that underpins the confidence that the dialogue partner needs to feel safe and thus achieve the development he or she wants. I revisit this topic in Chapter 9 in connection with a more detailed discussion of fundamental ways of being to promote transformative, fruitful, genuine and generative dialogues.

Being attentive of the problem, not the other's shortcomings

This topic and the focus of attention are addressed with inspiration from the narrative approach, with reference to the narrative therapists David Epston and Michael White's[17] famous statement: 'The problem is the problem, the person is not the problem'. In many cases, the troubled dialogue partner has internalized his or her problem: 'I *am* insecure!' That frames the problem as part of the person's identity, as a personality trait or feature. This fundamental shift in the way of examining the dialogue partner's challenges and problems places unique demands on the dialogue guide. It is up to the dialogue guide to *take the initiative to adopt a different focus of attention*, that is, to help the dialogue partner to stop seeing him/herself as a scapegoat, victim, helpless or powerless and instead support the person to view the problem from a different – liberating – angle. This new perspective is inspired by social-constructionist theory, which posits that reality is created in social interactions through the relationships we engage in, and thus the way we talk about the reality simultaneously shapes it.[18]

> In narrative practice the method that the dialogue guide applies to speak about the dialogue partner's problem in a different way is called an *externalizing conversation*. This means that the troubled dialogue partner speaks about the problem as something that is located *outside* him or her. The conversation refers to the problem in the third person. A case story may serve to illustrate the shift in the approach to the problem:

continued

---

16 Rogers, C. R. (1980). *A Way of Being*. Boston: Houghton Mifflin, p. 142.
17 Epston, D. & White, M. (1990). *Narrative Means to Therapeutic Ends*. New York: W.W. Norton.
18 See more in the lengthy Chapter 3.4.1 in Stelter (2012). *A Guide to Third Generation Coaching*. Berlin: Springer, pp. 92–132. It presents several social-constructionist approaches with a particular focus on coaching. And of course: Gergen, K. J. (2009). *Relational Being – Beyond Self and Community*. Oxford: Oxford University Press.

> Eve tells her good friend Ashley about her problem. Eve often feels very insecure in large groups of people. Ashley uses her narrative training, with Eve's consent, to ask a series of *externalizing questions* to help Eve consider her problem from a new perspective:
>
> - When did you feel that the insecurity began to dominate your life?
> - Are there specific types of situations where the insecurity overwhelms you?
> - Do you have any idea what intentions the insecurity has for you and your life?
> - If the insecurity had a voice, what would it be telling you?

These and similar questions gives the problem of *the insecurity* a voice, treating *the insecurity* as an actor with its own agency. The dialogue helps create some distance between the person and the problem, so that the person goes from feeling 'I am insecure' to thinking 'the insecurity has a plan and certain intentions in relation to me and my life' – a plan and intentions that it may be valuable to examine. By investigating the problem landscape in this light Eve, working with Ashley, discovers a new angle on the problem that has the potential to give Eve a new and very different understanding of her own situation. Attention to the problem and its plans, intentions, thoughts and feelings may have a liberating effect on Eve and other people with similar, difficult problems. The insecurity goes from being part of Eve's identity to being something that has a life of its own outside Eve. Externalizing the problem empowers the person to take action.

Enhancing attention to the ethical value perspective

Kierkegaard advocates the permanent striving for the ethical when he says:

> Therefore only when I look upon life ethically do I see it with regard to its beauty, only when I look upon my own life ethically do I see it with regard to its beauty. And if you say that this beauty is invisible, I reply, "In a sense it is in another sense it is not since it can be seen in the trace of the historical, seen as when it is said, *Loquere ut videam te*. True enough; what I see is not the consummation but the struggle, but I do see the struggle all the same, whenever I want to if I have the courage, and without courage I see nothing eternal at all, and consequently nothing beautiful either.[19]

By searching for beauty and reflecting on core values, words or concept the individual establishes a deep connection with him/herself and his or her

---

19 Kierkegaard, S. (1992). *Either/Or. A Fragment of Life*. London: Penguin Books, p. 562. (Original Danish edition 1843).

relationship with the world, which ultimately forms the basis of a capacity to act. In Chapter 5 the focus was on a fundamental understanding of the importance of values in a philosophical perspective and as a crucial basis of substance and meaning-making in the dialogue. In the following I discuss specific ways to incorporate a value perspective into the dialogue. Here, the *protreptic perspective* plays a key role – in a dialogue where the guide *orients his or her conversation partner(s)* (and him/herself) towards what matters most in life.

> As mentioned earlier, the dialogue can take its *point of departure in the abstract*, that is, a value, word or concept that frames an ethically founded conversation, where the interlocutors' mutual relationship gradually approach one of symmetry, as they engage on an abstract and universal human level. Another point of departure for the dialogue may be a specific situation, story or challenge where the dialogue guide *at an appropriate time takes the conversation to a discussion about values*. Here the focus is on narratives and on engaging in a conversation about specific challenges that revolve around certain unseen values, which can be actively brought to light in the context of the dialogues. A value-focused conversation is fairly loose and certainly not a manualized process. The dialogue guide asks questions that he or she would be able to answer him/herself, as a co-reflecting partner. Generally, Kirkeby describes the dialogue guide's/protreptician's required basic position as follows: 'That there is no other agenda than to encourage taking life seriously'. Protreptic value reflections seek to explore the universally human, which revolves around a certain concept or word. As the reflection unfolds, the dialogue partner's interest and engagement in the conversation becomes gradually clearer. The aim is to *discover the beauty* and the good intentions associated with the value concept that is being examined.

Structuring a conversation about values

As illustrated by Figure 4.1 in Chapter 4, *meaning* occupies the highest level in the hierarchy of intentionality. Reflections on values serve to unfold the underlying meaning in a selected concept (such as courage or agency). As a way of structuring this reflection on values the Copenhagen Coaching Center, which has particular expertise in protreptic dialogues, speaks, with inspiration from Aristotle, of *the logical cross*. This structuring concept forms the inspiration for the following presentation.[20]

---

20 Gørtz, K. & Mejlhede, M. (2015). *Protreptik i Praksis – Få Væsentlige Samtaler Til at Lykkes*. Copenhagen: Jurist- og Økonomforbundets Forlag. In my description I choose a practice-related terminology and thus deviate from the original terminology in the book. Another source of inspiration is Kirkeby (2015). *Protreptik – Selvindsigt og Samtalepraksis* – especially Chapter 30.2.

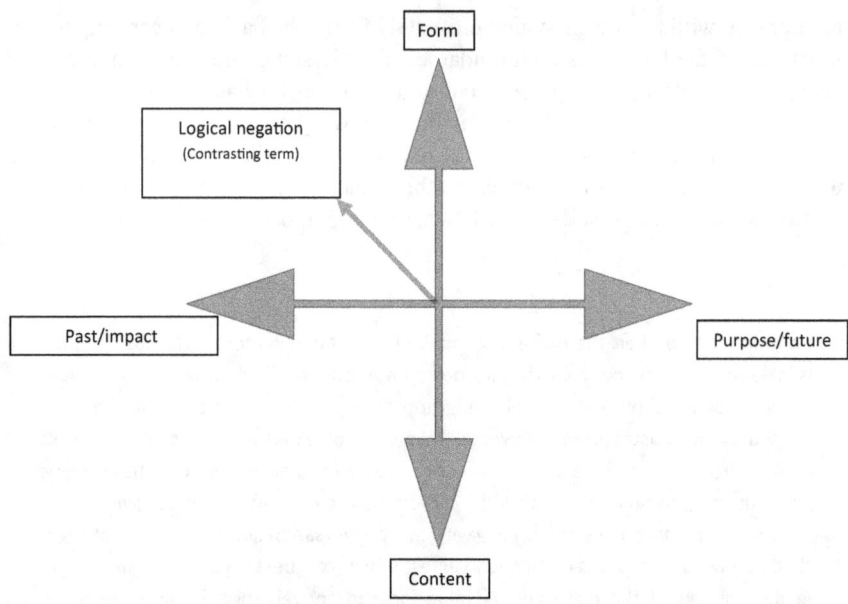

Figure 7.3 Examing a concept, a word or a value through the logical cross. (Illustration inspired by Gørtz & Mejlhede, 2015, p. 30.)

This approach operates with four dimensions, which may guide the reflection on the concept/value X – although the proptreptic reflection does not necessarily have to address all four aspects or proceed in any particular sequence:

1 *Past and impact*: Where does X come from? (This may include examining the etymological roots[21]). How did X come into being? What does X mean to you? What mood does X trigger in you? What feelings come up when you think of X? Do you associate anything in particular with X? How do you like the concept of X – what meaning does X hold for you?
2 *Form*: What is the form of X? How does X differ from the related concepts of Y and Z (for example 'courage' versus 'foolhardiness'; similarities and differences between 'credibility' and 'sincerity', 'honesty', 'guilelessness' or 'decency')?
3 *The logical negation in contrast to X as a specific category*: What is the opposite of X? What would the world be like if X did not exist? What is the downside of X?

In addition, Maibritt Isberg Andersen authored a small publication that was released in 2014: *Den Protreptiske Samtale – Din Håndbog*, which can be acquired, along with other practice-oriented material, from www.ztrong.dk.

21 A useful online source in English is www.etymonline.com.

4   *Content*: What does X consist of? For example, what form foes 'account-ability' take in your organization? What sort of *aura* or *appearance* does X have? How does X appear in you, when you feel good about yourself? What does X taste like? How does it smell? What colour is X? In what event or situation was X most clearly manifest? When is X (most clearly) present? What are the conditions for X to be manifest? How long can X last? What might be a threat to X?
5   *Purpose and future*: What is the purpose of X? What is going to happen to X? In what direction would the situation or you develop if X were fully expressed? What would be the best consequence of X for you/your organization/your project and so forth? What might influence X? How might X be expressed better or more?

In fact, this kind of protreptic dialogue may be viewed as an externalizing conversation, as the concept/value of X can also be viewed from the outside as an abstract or universal phenomenon. It is through this universally human approach to X that the dialogue brings forth moments of symmetry, as both/all participants in the dialogue can contribute to the reflection process.

Closing remarks

It takes great care and high ambitions to be a competent, trustworthy and empathic dialogue guide, whether in the role of coach, mentor, colleague or friend. I have highlighted *attention* as the most essential virtue for a fruitful, transformative and meaningful dialogue. The dialogue guide is not only directing attention to him/herself in his or her role as dialogue guide but always, and equally, to the other and the content aspects discussed above. This requires the ability to juggle several 'attention balls' at once. It is also important simply to be *present in the moment* without being distracted by one's own and others' expectations. The ability to engage in the other as an attentive and generous co-creative interlocutor is essential for a successful dialogue. Building a relationship with the other is absolutely crucial. I address this topic in Chapter 9.

Chapter 8

The narrative co-creative practice

Narrative practice is spreading to many practice fields and areas of society, including psychotherapy, psychiatry, nursing, medicine, social work, teaching and organizational development. In the postmodern world, meta-narratives or grand narratives have lost their value and their power of explanation. In the past, these narratives – many of them rooted in religion – helped provide a broadly accepted understanding of historical transformations and placed major events into a widely culturally accepted frame of reference. However, everyday 'small narratives', where people share uplifting events or difficulties, continue to play a pivotal role for everyone's desire to understand and share their world and their experiences with each other. Shaping narratives is the basis of social interaction, cultural development and – ultimately – being human and understanding ourselves in a larger context. Sharing narratives can have a healing impact or provide support for handling challenging life situations.

In this chapter I discuss how the dialogue participants' narrative-collaborative practice contributes to new understandings and insights, which lead to greater awareness, mutual respect and a sense of shared humanity. Sharing narratives helps develop social resilience and social capital.

Listening to the other's story – and telling your own

You probably have childhood memories of mom or dad reading bed-time stories to you. Listening to a story is an important experience for a child. We learn about the world through stories, we learn about others and we learn about ourselves. We form a community with the storyteller. We can talk about aspects of the story that move us. Hearing the story helps us find meaning in our own lives.[1] This insight into the value of storytelling increasingly informs practices within medicine, mediation, organization development, leadership and management,

1 Ingwersen, N. (1995). The need for narrative: the folktale as response to history. *Scandinavian Studies*, 67(1), 77–90.

evaluation, therapy and other forms of dialogues.[2] The practices that have developed within these different fields may look quite different. Narrative medicine[3] puts a high priority on listening to the patient's story in order to gain a better understanding of his or her health issues, general outlook and personal considerations in regard to illness and death, with the purpose of seeing the whole person behind the symptoms and the specific diagnosis. Narrative medicine also involves doctors' and other healthcare professionals' own stories to help them deal with the sadness they experience in connection with patient cases or ethical challenges they face. The narrative approach is shared in collegiate supervision situations in a hospital ward.

In the workplace, it may be more helpful for a supervisor to listen to an employee's story rather than simply pointing out sub-par performance or achievements. A broad understanding of the challenges faced by the employee may lead to a fruitful dialogue that revitalizes and renews the employee's motivation. The experience of being heard and understood can often move mountains and improve the employee's commitment and well-being.

One sign of the growing interest in narratives is the storytelling workshops that pop up around Denmark and around the world. Here, people share stories, socialize and learn about themselves and each other. A Danish folk high school advertises its storytelling workshop as follows:

> This course [storytelling workshop] is about bringing out your inner storyteller, and to do that, you need to get in touch with your own story. Your life and your story – your passion, your dreams and yearnings and the things that hold your fascination – are what give substance and zest to your story and your life![4]

In the following, the reader is introduced to narrative dialogue practice. When we engage with someone who is willing to listen and engage in the conversation, a story gradually begins to take form. This story is driven, in part, by the listener's comments, reflections and questions during the conversation. Thus, the conversation becomes a product of the interlocutors' co-creative and collaborative involvement

---

2   See, for example, Hühn, P., Pier, J., Schmid, W. & Schönert, J.. (2009). *Handbook of Narratology* (Narratologia: Contributions to Narrative Theory/Beiträge zur Erzähltheorie). Berlin, Germany: De Gruyter. About mediation, see Winslade, J. & Monk, Gerald D. (2013). *When Stories Clash: Addressing Conflict with Narrative Mediation*. Chagrin Falls, OH: Taos Institute Publications. About organization development, see Boje, D. (2008). *Storytelling Organizations*. London: SAGE. About management/leadership: Abramovitz, R. (2014). *Narrative Leadership: Leading with Elegance, Efficiency, and Efficacy*. Portland, OR: Sacred Circle Press. About narrative therapy, I recommend a short publication: Morgan, A. (2005). *What is Narrative Therapy?* Adelaide: Dulwich Centre. See a number of different books at: www.narrativeapproaches.com/bookshelf/.
3   Charon, R. (2006). *Narrative Medicine: Honoring the Stories of Illness*. New York, NY: Oxford University Press.
4   www.ronshoved.dk/fag/fortaellevaerksted [accessed 24 April 2016].

in the narrative process. One can also initiate a dialogue by preparing a written story that one wants to share with the other. The key is *how* the listener connects with what he or she hears. When someone invites one to listen to his or her story, it is essential to maintain a non-judging, unprejudiced stance and a keen interest in the story. In order to support the dialogue partner in his or her self-concept, narrative co-creative practice uses a so-called *statement of position map*,[5] which adds depth to the narrative. The narrative approach speaks of *thickening* the story. The statement of position map is used to address a specific problem in the following way:

Statement of position map

Naming
- What would you call the problem you are describing? Could you give the problem a name?

Effects
- How does [name of the problem] affect you? And others?
- How does it affect the way you and others act?

Evaluation
- How do you feel about the effects of [name of the problem] on you?
- How do you like it/not like it?
- Why/why not?
- Could there be a positive side to it?

Justification – values of the person
- Do you have a sense of why you feel the way you do about it?
- Why are you not happy with it? [This would be a good time to ask about values]
- Is there any aspect of it that you are happy with? What is your wish for your situation and your issue?
- In what way does your assessment of the situation differ from the way others see it?

The story represents one possible version of the world

In a transformative and fruitful dialogue inspired by narrative collaborative practice, the dialogue guide actively uses narratives to establish a co-creative partnership with the dialogue partner(s). In a transformative and fruitful dialogue

---

5 See Morgan, A. (2005). *What is Narrative Therapy?* Adelaide: Dulwich Centre Publications.

everyone has to feel secure and be open to developing and modifying their views, perceptions or understandings of the world in order to explore and uncover new aspects of themselves in relation to specific episodes. This has to involve new aspects that have not previously been the focus of attention. Stories always focus on a specific sequence of events with a view to conveying a particular point. The story relates one particular version of the world. Thus, any story has a plot or an action logic that enables the storyteller to highlight a particular point. The story is never 'the whole story'; we leave out incidents and events that do not align with the narrative plot – see the many Xs in Figure 8.1, which mark events in life that are not part of current storyline (the bold line). In his or her role as dialogue guide, the coach, for example, is a co-creator of new and, hopefully, more uplifting stories in cooperation with the dialogue partner. Figure 8.1 illustrates how the dialogue guide can help create a new and more uplifting story about a particular challenge that the dialogue partner is facing. The dialogue partner presents a story that has become a major source of stress for him or her. Consider Curt (see the case in Chapter 7), who no longer enjoyed going to work; in my conversation with him I arrived at an assumption that social interactions could become a uplifting element in his working life. Curt's storyline had been following a downward trend for some time (the second half of the bold line). As a dialogue guide I had the intention and desire to help Curt enjoy his working life more. My assumption about the role of socializing led to my key *exception question*, which was whether he might recall and describe a situation in his everyday life where

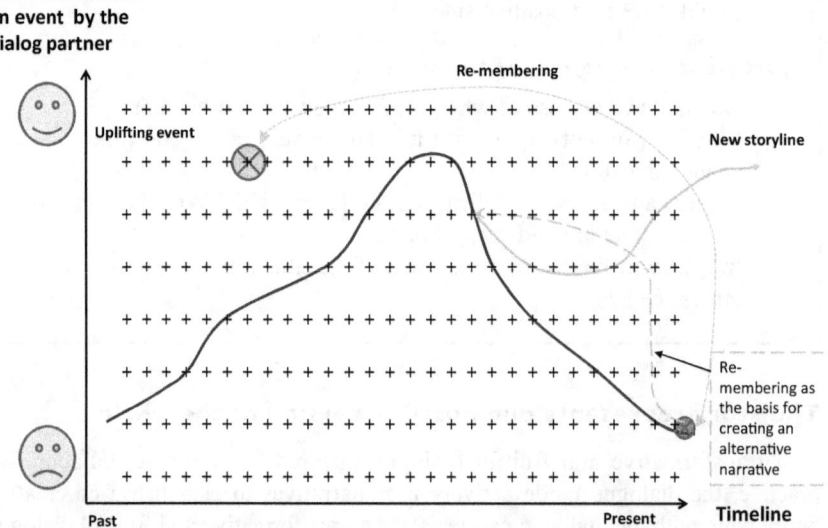

Figure 8.1 Reframing the story is made possible by the remembering of an earlier, uplifting event.

he actually enjoyed social interactions with others. With the exception question I sought, as a dialogue guide, to help my dialogue partner discover a specific event, which was more or less forgotten, but which the dialogue partner was able to recall in the context of our conversation. *Re-membering and recollecting* this uplifting event – being at the Skanderborg Festival with the lads – led to a new and more life-affirming alternative story of Curt's working life, where he may create and experience new moments of 'Skanderborg' in his working life (the new thin, rising storyline in Figure 8.1.).

A specific event that the dialogue guide seeks to highlight by asking the dialogue partner to consider exceptions or special, (almost) forgotten uplifting events can thus enable a new, rising storyline with a new plot. The uplifting exceptions can further form the basis of an examination with the use of the *statement of position map* mentioned above and with the use of the outsider witnessing staircase (see Figure 8.2): what influence might 'Skanderborg' actually have on your life? Why? What values do you attribute to 'Skanderborg' as an event? (*Evaluation)* Where does that take you with regard to your working life? What might 'Skanderborg' look like in your working life? (*Movement)*

The narrative collaborative and co-creative dialogue guide works from the basic assumption that narratives can be reframed and developed. This position lies in extension of social-constructionist theory, which defines our social reality as a result of the relationships we are part of or highlight in our stories. Another source of influence in this work is poststructuralist thinking, which embraces the possibility of multiple possible interpretations of a given text. The text or story can thus be deconstructed, developed and altered.

Co-creation in the dialogue

Several dialogue strategies from narrative, collaborative and co-creative practices can be employed to invite the dialogue partner to choose new perspectives on the stories that are being told and – if they are troubling or problematic – retold with an altered plot. In the following, I draw attention to the most co-creative activity in the dialogue partnership, where the dialogue guide acts as a fellow human being, accompanying the dialogue partner on his or her journey, and the two interlocutors position themselves in a mutual relationship that generates *moments of symmetry*. This is a new and innovative aspect that was presented with third-generation coaching, and which may be helpful in other everyday professional dialogues, where the dialogue guide actively adopts a co-creative position in relation to the dialogue partner(s) with the purpose of supporting and optimizing the reflective process. In group or team dialogues, any group member can adopt the role of co-creative partner. Moments of symmetry can occur when the dialogue guide or a group member shares reflections on specific descriptions, statements, feelings or thoughts from the focus person who has presented a specific challenge, which may also be shared by others in the group. This co-reflection by the dialogue guide or group member can be described as a form of *resonance*[6] with what the focus person says, a sounding board for the words, expressions or storylines that are presented. Hearing someone else's words constitutes a meeting, an exchange of experiences, feelings and thoughts where we not only respond to the other but also reflect on our own experiences, feelings and thoughts. For the dialogue guide or the members of the dialogue group, simply hearing the focus person's story can lead to a new understanding of one's own experiences and meaning-making. Thus, they receive a *gift* by listening. Sharing these experiences, thoughts and reflections can prove helpful for the dialogue partner. Thus, the dialogue guide or any other potential participants in turn give the focus person a *gift*. This creates a space for co-creative reflections and a shared understanding, where all the participants in the dialogue feel enriched and enlightened, as they reflect on each other's meaning-making and stories in light of their own meaning-making and stories. It is important to remember that the dialogue guide's or group members' contributions should encourage and contribute to new reflections and a new understanding for the focus person. An important concept in narrative co-creative practice is *outsider witnessing*, something that does not always occur in a systematic way in everyday dialogues. The key condition is to show humility and empathy. In an earlier publication I wrote:

> Witnessing is a method that is generally based on including others in the coachee's reflection process. White (2004) also speaks of defining ceremonies. The participants take turns to be audience and speaking actor. Someone witnesses what the coachee just said by reflecting on the coachee's statements in light of his or her own world view, values and everyday challenges. Witnessing serves as an element in the deconstruction of the coachee's existing reality, a reality that may be perceived as stressful, unsatisfactory or challenging. Witnessing by others aims to facilitate the coachee's re-construction of his or her reality, in part by means of thickened narratives that break with thin conclusions about the person's life, identity and relationships.[7]

The *outsider witnessing staircase* in Figure 8.2 can help the dialogue guide and any other group members acting as outsider witnesses and co-reflecting partners impose a more explicit structure to the co-creation process.

Some sample witnessing questions for the focus person, which may serve as inspiration for the dialogue guide or dialogue group members:

- What did you notice in the focus person's story? Which expression, which phrase captured your attention as a witness?

---

6 See more: Rosa, H. (2018). Resonance – *A Sociology of the Relationship to the World*. Oxford: Polity.
7 Stelter, R. (2012). *A Guide to Third Generation Coaching*, p. 135.

Narrative co-creative practice 103

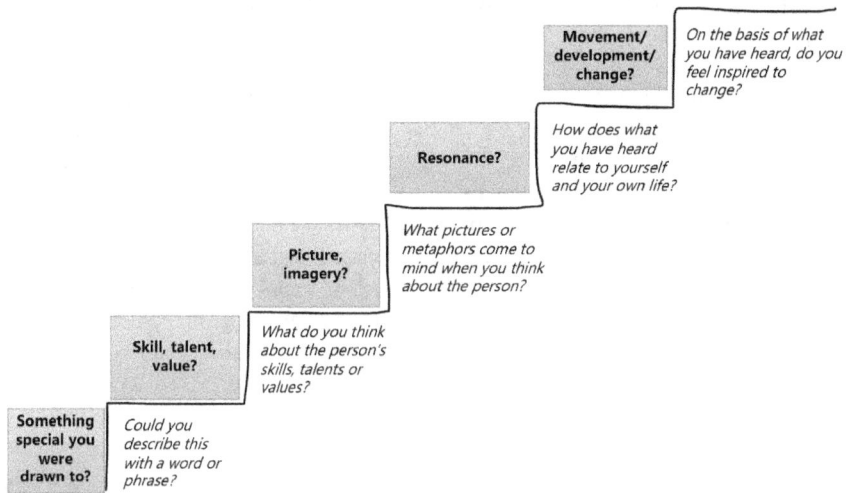

Figure 8.2 Outsider witnessing staircase.[8]

- What impression does it give you of the focus person's life, identity and the world in general? What does this expression/phrase tell you about the person's intentions, values, beliefs, aspirations and commitments?
- What does this expression/phrase tell you if you relate it to your own life? What thoughts does it initiate in you? What are your thoughts on it?
- How does the focus person's story move you? Where has your experience of the story taken you?

Chené Swart, a narrative coach and organization developer from South Africa, describes the experience of being touched and moved by the tale of the other as a *gift*. Swart offers the following description:

> When listening to a story teller, narrative practitioners are always aware that they are not only witnessing a story, but in the listening their lives are also touched by the story of the other. This point of being moved and touched by the story being listened to, I have come to call *gifts*. Gifts can be learnings from a story, a reminder of my own values and beliefs which I may have forgotten, a challenge to my own beliefs and ideas about something, an experience of not being alone in my own struggles and thoughts, and so forth.[9]

---

8 The figure is inspired by training material from the Copenhagen Coaching Center.
9 Swart, C. (2013). *Re-Authoring the World: The Narrative Lens and Practices for Organisations, Communities and Individuals*. Bryanston, JHB, South Africa: Knowledge Resources, p. 168.

Sharing one's reflections with the dialogue partners means receiving or giving a gift:

1. By highlighting certain words and phrases that were used by the focus person and by reflecting on one's own experiences and possible challenges, the dialogue guide *receives the gift* of becoming more aware of his or her own feelings, thoughts or challenges.
2. By reflecting the statements back to the focus person, the dialogue guide *gives* the focus person *a gift*. In that sense, the dialogue guide or dialogue group member may ideally be able to use the focus person's story as a valuable contribution that helps the focus person reinterpret and achieve a deeper understanding of the challenge that he or she is grappling with.

Receiving and giving gifts is a beautiful metaphor that illustrates the value of the co-creative and collaborative character of dialogues or third-generation coaching. Narrative collaborative and co-creative dialogues can breathe new life into a dialogue format that seems more necessary than ever before, in today's hypercomplex world where people need inspiration and shared reflection to be able to handle specific challenges in their personal and working lives. Receiving and giving gifts means sharing insights and finding meaning together. Hypercomplexity involves recognizing multicultural perspectives and thus understanding the many different ways of finding meaning in the world. Figure 8.3 illustrates how a dialogue guide can serve as an outsider witness who either receives or gives a gift. Narrative co-creative dialogues take form on the basis of the dialogue partner's descriptions, statements and reflections in relation to:

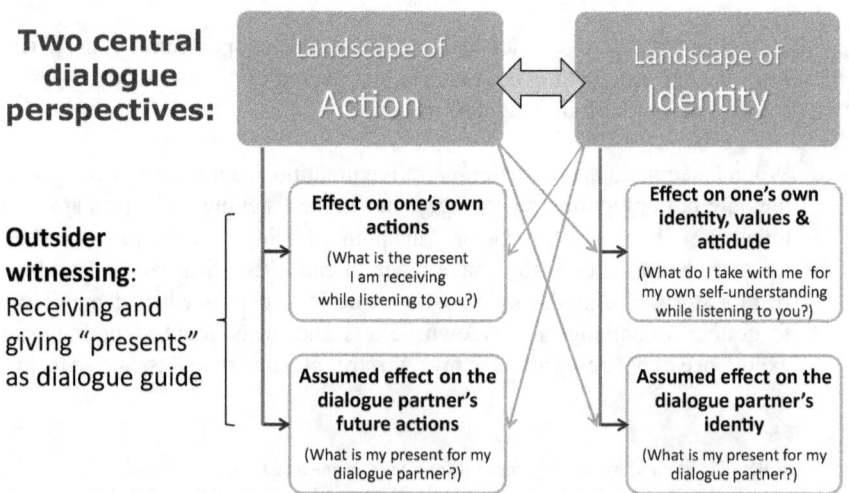

Figure 8.3 Outsider witnessing procedure as a process of receiving and giving 'gifts'.

- Specific acts/activities (addressed as *action landscapes*, for example: 'Recently, as I was starting up a new project that was fairly complicated, I was able to organize my team in a way that helps us all work with renewed focus and energy . . .').
- Specific personal beliefs, attitudes, values, dreams, intentions, expectations and so forth. (These are addressed as *identity landscapes*, for example: 'I think it's absolutely crucial to have a good climate in the team').

Figure 8.3 illustrates how the outsider witness (the dialogue guide or a group member) takes his or her point of departure in the dialogue partner's statements, which in turn relate back to the action or identity landscape. The figure outlines how a dialogue guide or dialogue group member can act as a co-reflecting partner. Thus, the interlocutors approach a position of symmetry in the dialogue, where they share a humane, compassionate and co-reflecting stance. The figure should be seen as a structure for giving and receiving gifts in the co-creative dialogue.

In the therapy literature, outsider witnessing is often compared to self-disclosure, although the two terms have somewhat different meanings. Psychotherapy recognizes the benefits of self-disclosure as well as the potential risks.[10] The co-creative dialogue practice presented here emphasizes the *exchange of gifts* – as described in Figure 8.3 – as a particular form of self-disclosure interaction and as a valuable element that strengthens the working alliance between dialogue guide and dialogue partners. In psychotherapy, self-disclosure has been found to promote empathy and facilitate immediate results.[11] It is, however, important to underscore how important it is that self-disclosure and self-involvement not exclusively serve the dialogue guide's needs, as that would only remove the focus from the dialogue partner looking for help, who would find this kind of self-involvement from the other strange or annoying. This reminder cannot be over-emphasized. Outsider witnessing and the exchange of gifts also has a somewhat different aim than the aim of self-disclosure in psychotherapy. Exchanging gifts not only serves the purpose of ensuring a good atmosphere in the dialogue. It promotes a degree of reciprocity in our understanding and invites different perspectives into the conversation; new perspectives that first of all help the dialogue partner, who is seeking help, develop and find new mean-ing and new narratives about him/herself, specific events and, ultimately, his or her life.

Symmetry in the dialogue

Striving for moments of symmetry in the dialogue is the perspective and the ambition that distinguishes third-generation coaching from traditional understand-

---

10 Sturges, J. W. (2012). Use of therapist self-disclosure and self-involving statements. *The Behavior Therapist*, 35(5), 90–93.
11 Norcross, J. C. (2010). The therapeutic relationship. In Duncan, B. L., Miller, S. D., Wampold, B. B. E. & Hubble, M. A. (eds.) (2010). *The Heart & Soul of Change* (2nd edition) (pp. 113–141). Washington, DC: American Psychological Association.

ings of coaching and other supportive dialogue forms – from therapy to counselling. Symmetry can best be developed and sought in a community of practice where all the interlocutors have a shared interest in change – in their own lives and in the world they live in. The partners strive for insight and new knowledge, albeit often without having a clear goal in sight, due to the growing complexity of many issues. Full symmetry will never be possible, however; between one or two participants there are bound to be differences with regard to the knowledge or rhetorical skill they show in the dialogue. However, by developing a community of practice they can approach a shared understanding that helps them to move on – in accordance with the motto of third-generation coaching: *In true dialogue both sides are willing to change.*[12]

Moments of symmetry in the practice community

There is a certain theory about communities of practice that was originally developed in the intersection of anthropology and adult learning.[13] In this theory, learning is defined as an aspect of many different situations in people's personal and working life, as people supplement each other and contribute to the community. No member of a practice community has the sort of knowledge monopoly that would once have been held by a school teacher or a workplace manager. In the community of practice, some members will be more peripheral than others who, due to their experience, background, skills or commitment, occupy a more central position. Thus, there will always be some degree of asymmetry. These relative positions will, however, vary with the task and the challenges at hand. Some individuals who have been at the periphery move closer to the centre if the focus shifts to a field where their skills, experiences or commitment play a more essential role. Knowledge is developed in the given context through shared practice and dialogues in the situation and in relation to specific tasks or topics. A community of practice, from two members to an entire department, is characterized by three key elements:[14]

- *Mutual engagement*: The basis of mutual engagement is that the members are able to *supplement each other*. Their overlapping competencies lay the strongest foundation for the development of a functioning practice community. Their interaction is characterized by mutual relationships, which always involve situations with a varying degree of relational symmetry.
- *A joint enterprise* helps build team spirit and is based on a dialogue culture, where diversity and co-creation form the basis of a collective development

12 This sentence is printed as a quote by Thich Nhat Hanh on the title page of Stelter, R. (2012).
13 Lave, J. & Wenger, E. (1991). *Situated Learning. Legitimate Peripheral Participation.* Cambridge, UK: Cambridge University Press.
14 Wenger, E. (2004). *Communities of Practice. Learning, Meaning, and Identity.* Cambridge, UK: Cambridge University Press.

process that continuously involves all the members in one form or another. All the members are involved in co-creating their shared reality, where mutual trust and both individual and shared responsibility are important conditions for learning and development.
- *A shared repertoire* develops and changes over time through a joint enterprise that is pursued in a team, department and so forth and contains routines, concepts, tools, action strategies, conversation forms, stories, discourses, gestures, symbols and certain ways of doing things. Here, co-creative dialogues can be an important repertoire for the further development of an existing community of practice.

A community of practice is thus not something that merely exists: it needs to be established by some form of agreement or contract and maintained and nurtured through the topics and tasks that inherently legitimize the existence of the community. Over time, a culture develops in the community that is most clearly expressed in the shared repertoire that the community produces. In a one-on-one relationship, as it is found in coaching or other transformative dialogues and development talks, establishing a fruitful space by introducing an appropriate framework and contract is crucial for the development potential of the relationship. In larger communities, too, it is important to establish legitimacy and a context for the membership – for example a purpose for the existence of a team or a job description that defines the membership criterion. Symmetry in a relationship or community will never last long, but may arise in specific moments, as the members come together in shared meaning-making in relation to the task or the topic at hand.

We experience symmetry when we feel understood and touched by another as we develop or discuss something in close interaction around the meaning we co-create. This could be a specific task where the members really *supplement each other*, and where nobody can quite tell who contributes what. *The joint enterprise* moves into the foreground. In these situations the members may experience *flow*, a sense of vitalizing engagement, complete focus and involvement and maximum satisfaction while they are immersed in the activity. It is a state where involvement in the task or the dialogue is the ultimate goal.[15]

In everyday professional dialogues, where the focus is often on reflecting on specific job tasks and interaction patterns and, ultimately, on completing tasks and improving relationships, a higher degree of equality and symmetry is crucial for improving productivity and well-being in the organization. It is thus essential to qualify these everyday professional dialogues to ensure that they are

---

15 The concept of and thinking about flow was developed by M. Csikszentmihalyi in the book *Flow. The Psychology of Optimal Experience*. New York, NY: Harper and Row, 1990. Flow was later associated with the movement of positive psychology. A newer book unfolds the topic even more: Csikszentmihalyi, M. (2013). *Creativity: Flow and the Psychology of Discovery and Invention*. New York: HarperCollins Publisher.

transformative and fruitful. To that end, many members of the organization should be empowered and trained to act as dialogue guides, and the organization as a whole should strive to develop a *coaching* and *co-creative and collaborative dialogue culture* that makes room for agency, creativity, job satisfaction and the whole person.

Moments of symmetry in the reflection on values

Protreptic reflections offer room and opportunity for symmetry. A focus on certain values that are addressed in the community enables the members to move beyond the concrete level by relating to each other in a more 'abstract' sense and to the task or topic that forms the foundation of their cooperation and existence as a team. A community of practice is based on collective *meaning-making* and thus on certain specific values, which become part of their shared repertoire. These values will normally develop through the way they act to achieve specific tasks, which form the basis and legitimacy of the community. In some situations it will be helpful if the community – for example, a department in an organization – picks up on a special initiative from an individual to focus on specific values that are considered to be crucial for the community.

In one-on-one relationships, for example in coaching and other everyday and transformative dialogues, one could similarly focus on a particular concept or value, for example by asking: what does 'agency' or 'courage' mean to you? Normally, one of the parties will be the main initiator or driver of the conversation. Nevertheless, over time, moments of symmetry will emerge in the conversation, precisely because the dialogue unfolds on a universally human level, and because the value in question – courage, for example – also holds importance for the dialogue guide. Striving for the *abstract*, the *universally human* generates an unknown dynamic in the conversation where the interlocutors meet at a level that they do not experience in conversations that are focused on a specific situation or act. Thus, protreptic value reflections form the kind of conversation that, despite any professional asymmetry (such as that which exists between a leader and an employee), it is characterized by a universal humanity, equality and moments of symmetry that do not occur in conversation that deal strictly with specific challenges or practice situations.

Closing remarks

Telling a story to someone and listening to a rich or *thickened* story will always be inspiring for people who matter to one another. In a professional dialogue context, an extra dimension is added. Here, a person contacts a dialogue guide in order to sort something out or to seek help and support to deal with a difficult issue. This gives the dialogue guide the special task of helping to deconstruct the story that has been told and to help create something new, adding a new plot to the story that the focus person can live with and use for personal development and to develop his or her situation in a fruitful direction. To be available to the other, to empathize with the other and to act as a sounding board in a shared search for new understanding constitute the dialogue guide's core ambition. New and uplifting stories emerge in a community of practice, whether this community involves only two persons or a larger group or team.

Chapter 9

The foundation of dialogue and the dialogue guide's virtues

Shaping dialogue is an art. Ideally, the dialogue should take place in the context of a well-defined framework and a safe environment. Transformative and fruitful dialogues require an agreement and a contract, where both parties settle their respective positions in the conversation, and where they show the willingness, engagement and ambition to be worthy of their mutual meeting. Research within the fields of psychotherapy and coaching underscores the importance and meaning of the relationship and the dialogue guide's abilities and virtues as the foundation of a successful dialogue. In connection with this discussion, in this chapter I present research on common factors and their consequences for the way the dialogue is conducted. I present and discuss the main ingredients and ways of being that are necessary for the art of dialogue.

Art is by definition a creative activity. The art of dialogue goes beyond that, as it is a collaborative and co-creative activity. The art of dialogue requires something special: it takes (at least) two to tango. The dialogue guide lays a good foundation via his or her engagement and faith in the dialogue partner, while the dialogue partner acts as part of the dialogue partnership through his or her active participation and desire to develop.

Clarifying concepts and conditions for transformative dialogues

From an etymological perspective the term 'dialogue' is quite broad. In the present context, 'dialogue' is understood with its original Greek denotation: *dialogue* = across, through, throughout (διά/diá) combined with speech, meaning, discourse (λόγος/lógos). The participants in the dialogue develop a mutual relationship through speech and the discourse that unfolds in their relationship. I am not speaking here of negotiation, argumentation or debate; instead, I wish to look at *everyday professional dialogues* or *transformative dialogues* as a conversation art where the dialogue guide relates simultaneously to him/herself and to the other. When the purpose is to give rise to something new, the focus of the dialogue must be on the newness that can emerge between the interlocutors.

In the present context I speak broadly of transformative dialogues, which include, among other things, professional conversations, coaching and mentoring, and which can be described as a form of conversation where the dialogue guide acts as a *fellow human being*.[1] In light of this dialogical and co-creative approach, the psychotherapeutic term 'intervention' should be avoided. To intervene essentially means 'to come between, to interrupt'[2] and suggests a medical mindset, where the focus is on dysfunctions in the patient or client, and where it is up to the doctor to come up with a problem-solving treatment.[3] Intervention may thus be interpreted as an act where a professional does something *to* someone. This understanding is quite far from the collaborative and co-creative partnership that is suggested by the term 'transformative dialogues'. The prominent coaching scholar and practitioner Erik de Haan instead recommends that we speak of *interaction* rather than intervention. He proposes a list of 'ten commandments' for the executive coach, which I include here in a modified version for your inspiration.[4] I have expanded the focus with some supplemental comments in order to give the guidelines broad appeal and make them applicable to any kind of transformative dialogue. The 'commandments' are based on research studies of *common factors*, which I present in greater detail later in this chapter, and which can shed light on many types of conversations. My intention is to help you get started as a dialogue guide and to offer a framework that does not merely consist of expert tips but actually constitutes evidence-based guidelines. The key requirements are to be motivated by good intentions, to wish the best for the dialogue partner, to be clear about one's own professional boundaries and to be fully focused and present in the conversation. The ten 'commandments' include ethical considerations,[5] provide a basic orientation for practice and identify the most important professional positions. I recommend that you study these guidelines, reflect on them, discuss and interpret them together with a colleague and take ownership of your own understanding of them.

> 1 First, do no harm! It is better to do too little than to do harm.
> 2 Have confidence! As long as you are guided by ethical principles and sincere intentions, you can actually make a difference.

---

1 See also: Stelter, R. (2016). The coach as a fellow human companion. In L. E. van Zyl, M. W. Stander & A. Odendaal (eds.), *Coaching Psychology: Meta-Theoretical Perspectives and Applications in Multi-Cultural Contexts* (pp. 47–66). Basel: Springer.
2 Cf. *Online Etymology Dictionary* www.etymonline.com, look-up: intervention.
3 See also http://medical-dictionary.thefreedictionary.com/medical+model [accessed 11 May 2016].
4 See de Haan, E. (2008). *Relational Coaching – Journey Towards Mastering One-to-One Learning*. Chichester: Wiley, pp. 47–51. In my discussion of these 'commandments' I replace the term 'coachee' with 'dialogue partner' in order to indicate a broader application.
5 See, for example, *EMCC's Global Code of Ethics*: www.emccouncil.org/src/ultimo/models/Download/4.pdf.

3 Commit yourself heart and soul to your approach! Showing commitment, confidence, attachment and loyalty to your approach can make a difference. Read from any missteps and the feedback you receive.
4 Feed the hope of your dialogue partner! Hope is a crucial factor in development and change. Help your dialogue partner to embrace hope!
5 Consider the coaching situation from your dialogue partner's perspective! Your dialogue partner's expectations influence the effectiveness of your relationship. Ask for feedback from your dialogue partner as the process unfolds!
6 Work on your coaching relationship! When you have a good relationship, there is a good chance that the dialogue will have a positive effect.
7 If you don't 'click', find a replacement coach! A good match based on mutual trust and respect is the foundation of a fruitful dialogue.
8 Look after yourself, to keep yourself as healthy as possible! It seems to make a difference for the positive development of the dialogue that you, as the dialogue guide, appear attractive, competent, stable, healthy, happy, empathic, warm and reliable.
9 Try to stay fresh and unbiased! Rigid procedures and protocols are not helpful but counterproductive.
10 Don't worry too much about the specific things you are doing! Be present in the moment! Use your personal strengths, and make yourself available as a good conversation partner.

To clarify the research basis of these ten guidelines I will briefly outline the research findings that are summarized under the category of *common factors*.

Research into common factors

Awareness of the so-called common or non-specific factors took on a prominent role in psychotherapy research, where it became clear that several different techniques and approaches can have a positive effect on therapy outcomes.[6] Therapeutic practice often relies on a mix of approaches. Research has identified

---

6 Here I refer to Lambert, M. J. & Barley, D. E. (2002). Research summery on therapeutic relationship and psychotherapy outcome. In J. Norcross (ed.), *Psychotherapy Relationships that Work*, pp. 17–32. Oxford: Oxford University Press; Laska, K., Gurman, A., Wampold, B. & Hilsenroth, M. J. (2014). Expanding the lens of evidence-based practice in psychotherapy: a common factors perspective. *Psychotherapy*, 51(4), 467–481; Miller, S., Hubble, M. & Duncan, B. (2007). *Supershrinks: What is the Secret of Their Success?* www.psychotherapy.com.au/fileadmin/site_files/pdfs/Supershrinks.pdf (retrieved 24 Feb. 2018); Wampold, B. E. (2010). The research evidence for common factors models: A historically situated perspective. In: B. L. Duncan, S. D. Miller, B. E. Wampold & M. A. Hubble (eds.), *The Heart & Soul of Change: Delivering What Works in Therapy*. (2nd edition), pp. 49–81. Washington, DC: American Psychological Association.

certain common factors that all good therapists and all good dialogue situations have in common and has found these factors to have a crucial impact on the positive outcome of the conversations. In recent years, additional studies have examined the role of common factors in coaching.[7]

Studies have documented that the following common factors promote the conversation's positive impact on the dialogue partner who is seeking help and on the outcome of the process – also outside the field of therapy:[8]

Social network factors

These are factors within the social context of the person seeking support (for example in the organization, family, social circle) that have a key impact on the long-term outcome of the conversation. Thus, what happens not only depends on the person who is seeking help but also, and perhaps even more so, on the context of his or her personal and working life. Among the important social network factors are core values, social support, supportive knowledge, procedures and guidelines and the dialogue partner's (client's) recognition of the value of the conversation.

Dialogue guide factors

The dialogue guide's *way of being* in the conversation makes an important contribution to the outcome. This includes the dialogue guide's own well-being, authenticity, empathy and acceptance of the dialogue partner's situation.

Client factors

The client or dialogue partner's engagement and involvement frame the third group of factors: a sense of concern and need and an active search for help play an important role in framing the conversation. Hope and an expectation of change form an important perspective. The person who is seeking support has to perceive the dialogue guide as credible for the conversation to develop in a fruitful and transformative manner.

---

7 Two new studies should be mentioned here: de Haan, E., Duckworth, A., Birch, D., Jones, C. & Lowman, Rodney L. (2013). Executive coaching outcome research: the contribution of common factors such as relationship, personality match, and self-efficacy. *Consulting Psychology Journal: Practice and Research*, 65(1), 40–57 and Gessnitzer, S. & Kauffeld, S. (2015). The working alliance in coaching. *The Journal of Applied Behavioral Science*, 51(2), 177–197.

8 Inspiration for this overview drew on Cameron, M. (2014). This is common factors. *Clinical Social Work Journal*, 42, 151–160. For a comparison of common factors in psychotherapy in relation to other social interaction processes, see Lampropoulos, G. K. (2001). Common processes of change in psychotherapy and seven other social interactions. *British Journal of Guidance & Counselling*, 29(1), 21–33.

Relational factors

The form of the relationship itself is foundational for a positive dialogue process: Both parties are encouraged to engage in the relationship and in the change and development process. Productive and fruitful direct and indirect communication and good cooperation between the parties are important for building a successful relationship. A common understanding of the problem, tasks and purpose/goal and of the distribution of roles promotes a good relationship and thus increases the likelihood of a positive outcome.

Practice strategies

Any transformative and fruitful dialogue is based on a change rationale (for example inspired by third-generation coaching), where the dialogue guide has faith in the positive effect of the dialogue. Specific dialogue strategies also play a key role – this includes approaches to reflection, feedback, wondering, attention, insight, emotional learning, knowledge, information sharing, the development and testing of new ways of acting, success and mastery experiences, appreciation and suggestions and the dialogue guide's way of offering support.

The reflective practitioner

The research findings about common factors outlined above encourage us to include the entire context as an important dimension that shapes the development process. If the focus person's organization (for example team leaders, executives and co-workers) or general life context are not going to be available to offer supportive follow-up with regard to the development ambitions that are pursued in the dialogue, an otherwise satisfactory or successful outcome may fail. Social support and the social network around the person are essential for progress and change. The individual is rarely able to move forward alone, without support from his or her surroundings.

It is also important to be a trusting and supportive dialogue partner who has the development of the relationship and the interaction as a top priority. The research outlined earlier shows that the dialogue guide's ability and virtues with regard to connecting with another person in dialogue are at least as relevant as his or her skill in using the selected approach. Especially when we move beyond psychotherapy and towards practicing other everyday professional dialogues, I see third-generation coaching as a valuable source of inspiration for collaborative and co-creative conversations – especially due to its fundamentally undogmatic and relational orientation. In the art of lingering in dialogue, it is the meaning- and value-oriented collaboration between the dialogue participants that determines the transformative impact of the dialogue. The dialogue partner has to be able to link the chosen dialogue approach with an ability to include and attend to the common factors outlined above, with their emphasis on the relational dimension of the interaction. A key factor in the dialogue guide's own development is the ability to reflect on his or her own practice. Schön describes the reflective practitioner's ability as follows:

> It is our capacity to *see-as* and *act-as* that allows us to have a feel for problems that do not fit existing rules. The artistry of a practitioner ... hinges on the range and variety of the repertoire that he brings to unfamiliar situations. Because he is able to *see* these *as* elements of his repertoire, he is able to make sense of their uniqueness and need not reduce them to instances of standard categories.[9]

Clearly, dialogue can be a highly complex practice that is more of an art than a skill. It is not always easy to translate the many theories, principles and instructions presented in relevant books into practice. Practice is complex, wide-ranging, surprising and often very different from the clear-cut, idealized image conveyed by theory. Confidence and common sense are two key ingredients of a good dialogue. Schön points to the spontaneous, intuitive performance of everyday acts as the basis of his subsequent conclusion, which leads to the concept of *reflection-in-action*: 'Our knowing is ordinarily implicit in our patterns of action and in our feel for the stuff with which we are dealing'.[10] The key factor in developing our professional dialogue practice is the ability to reflect on our practice in order to develop our skill and competence as supportive practitioners.[11]

Reflection-in-action – reflection-on-action

Reflection-in-action should be understood as part of the dialogue. Reflection-in-action is thus a shared project for both parties in the dialogue relationship – a *reflection-in-interaction*. Here, clear agreements, continuous follow-up and mutual feedback and co-reflection play a key role. With inspiration from a group of psychotherapists under the umbrella of the American Psychological Association I am going to introduce the ideas behind Feedback-Informed Treatment, FIT,[12] which underscores the importance of the cooperation that leads to a successful dialogue format and, potentially, a successful outcome. They highlight three dimensions of FIT, which I have adapted to everyday professional conversations by incorporating Schön's reflective practitioner thinking:

---

9 Schön, D. A. (1983). *The Reflective Practitioner. How Professionals Think in Action*. New York, NY: Basic Books, p. 140.
10 Ibid. p. 49.
11 Stelter, R. (2014). *A Guide to Third Generation Coaching* has much more about practitioner research and reflective practices in Chapter 6, which is only outlined briefly here.
12 See for further information: Prescott, D., Maeschalck, Cynthia L, Miller, Scott D. & American Psychological Association issuing body. (2017). *Feedback-Informed Treatment in Clinical Practice, Reaching For Excellence*. Washington, DC: American Psychological Association.

1   *Create a culture of feedback, of reflection-in-interaction!* It is important to clarify the dialogue guide's ambition at the outset of the conversation or cooperation process as part of the contract that is established between the interlocutors. A brief feedback round during and toward the end of a conversation can help drive the dialogues forward and clear up any misunderstandings.
2   *Integrate feedback and the dialogue participants' reflections in the way you continue the conversation!* Co-creative dialogue is based on collaboration. Integrating the dialogue partner's ideas, reflections and feedback helps develop the relationship and gives the dialogue partner a productive shared responsibility for developing the dialogue. The dialogue guide will be able to receive a great deal of important information for his or her further development as a dialogue guide.
3   *Learn to fail successfully!* Practice makes perfect! Any misunderstandings between the interlocutors and any adjustments you make, as the dialogue guide, will only make you stronger and more competent over time.

Tilsen and McNamee offer an interesting supplement, which can be adapted in the spirit of third-generation coaching, describing

> FIT as an elaboration of social construction in that it: (1) recognizes all models and methods of therapy as discursive options—all offer viable "languages" for engagement—based on the pragmatics of how well a particular practice allows us to go on [. . .]; and (2) involves the reflexive practice of inviting feedback into the therapeutic relationship to co-construct emergent meaning with clients.[13]

When FIT, as a continuous process of reflection and collaboration, is successful it increases the intensity of the relationship, which generally facilitates the overall dialogue process and promotes a positive and rewarding outcome of the conversation or dialogue process.

Achieving depth in the conversation – being on the other's terms

In the following I will elaborate on certain key aspects of the dialogue. By emphasizing these aspects I hope to help you develop a sense of the depth of the dialogue. Mutual understanding and empathy with the dialogue partner are important requirements for making the communication what it should be to live up to the true meaning of the word: a connection between two human beings. When moments of meeting occur in a conversation they are the exception rather

---

13   Tilsen, J. & McNamee, S. (2015). Feedback informed treatment. evidence-based practice meets social construction. *Family Process*, 54(1), p. 130.

than the norm. Everyday communication is often characterized by misunderstandings, lack of empathy and rare moments of true mutual understanding. Such is life. Fundamentally, every human being is an autonomous being with his or her own perspective on and view of the world. Etymologically, the word 'communication' means to 'share', 'join', 'unite', 'make common'.[14] To communicate means to create a basis for people to share understanding and meaning. That is an ambition that depends on each individual's ability to empathize with the other's life world. As mentioned in Chapter 7, I adopt Ole Fogh Kirkeby's neologism *heteroenticity* – 'being on the other's behalf and on the other's terms'. It is a key position for any dialogue guide aiming to achieve depth in a conversation.

In the following I introduce two concepts that help you achieve the necessary depth and interaction in the communication promote mutual understanding.[15]

Withness-thinking

The English communication theorist John Shotter proposed the concept of *withness-thinking* to describe the in-depth character of the dialogue. In his writings Shotter generally seeks to link the social-constructionist and the phenomenological position; an ambition that I share. Through the dialogue the interlocutors develop a shared reality by listening to and exchanging ideas, thoughts and experiences based on their individual understanding and meaning-making. The concept of *withness-talk* or *withness-thinking* seeks to describe this intense meeting with the other as follows:

> Withness (dialogic)-talk/thinking occurs in those reflective interactions that involve our coming into living, interactive contact with an other's living being, with their utterances, with their bodily expressions, with their words, their 'works'. It is a meeting of outsides, of surfaces, of two kinds of 'flesh' . . ., such that they come into 'touch' or 'contact' with each other. . . . In the interplay of living movements intertwining with each other, new possibilities of relation are engendered, new interconnections are made, new 'shapes' of experience can emerge.[16]

The key point in this excerpt is the emphasis placed on *coming into contact with* another. In an age with growing amounts of hyper-information, where we usually only receive messages and, perhaps, 'likes' via social media, it becomes important to *linger* in one's own and the other's thinking. To share each other's

---

14 See 'communication' at www.etymonline.com.
15 Both concepts were previously presented in Stelter, R. (2014). *A Guide to Third Generation Coaching*. Berlin: Springer.
16 Shotter, J. (2006). Understanding process from within: An argument for witness-thinking. Organization Studies, 27(5), 600. The word 'flesh' is a reference to Merleau-Ponty (1968).

thoughts or reflections in a trusting and empathic way is crucial for the quality of the dialogue and for a successful relationship between the dialogue participants. *Coming into contact* can be compared with *being empathic*, which in my understanding can be described as being passionate on behalf of the other and feeling with the other. Carl Rogers remains one of the leading figures in the field of psychological counselling and psychotherapy. He highlighted the role of empathy as a key element in psychological counselling and offered the following definition:

> [Being empathic] means entering the private perceptual world of the other and becoming thoroughly at home in it. It involves being sensitive, moment to moment, to the changing felt meanings which flow in this other person. . . . It means temporarily living in his/her life, moving about in it delicately without making judgments . . . It includes communicating your sensings of his/her world . . .[17]

In this excerpt, Rogers's phenomenological outlook is evident. He used the term *felt meaning* to describe a meeting place for therapist and client. The term 'felt meaning' or *felt sense* also points back to Gendlin, who is currently known for his focusing approach.[18] (See also Chapter 7). Felt meaning or felt sense may be observed and applied as a possible point of departure for the dialogue partner's profound understanding of certain events in his or her life. When the dialogue partner understands his or her felt meaning and shares this understanding with the dialogue guide, both parties need a close connection, which involves elements of withness-thinking and withness-talk, and where the dialogue guide strives to meet and understand his or her dialogue partner's life universe.

Relational attunement

This intensive meeting can further be described as a form of *relational attunement* between the dialogue participants. Their partnership hinges on both parties demonstrating a willingness to engage with the other, to show mutual empathy and sympathy. The purpose of the dialogue is to develop a focused presence and attunement where the participants continuously seek to 'tune in to' each other's thinking, feelings and reflections. This process in turn leads to something other and more: as one listens to the other's story, one can simultaneously attend to oneself and the sensations, feelings and thinking that the story produces in one's

---

17 Rogers, C. (1975). Empathic – an unappreciated way of being. *The Counseling Psychologist*, 5(2), 3; the article is available online at www.sageofasheville.com/pub_downloads/EMPATHIC_AN_UNAPPRECIATED_WAY_OF_BEING.pdf [retrieved 20 Feb. 2018].
18 See Gendlin, E. T. (1982). *Focusing*. (2nd edition). New York, NY: Bantam Books. Gendlin, E. T. (1996). *Focusing-Oriented Psychotherapy*. New York/London: The Guilford Press. Gendlin, E. T. (1997). *Experiencing and the Creation of Meaning*. Evanston, IL: Northwestern University Press (original from 1962).

own mind. Finally, relational attunement also involves reflecting back what one has heard and how it may have affected oneself. We *wonder* about what we hear, share our questions with each other and try, together, to find meaning – through dialogue. From this perspective, *relational attunement* can be defined as:

> a *shared or co-created articulation*, where a sensation, a sensory impression or a theme is addressed collectively, and where the participants achieve a meeting. People become each other's sounding boards. Relational attunement generates new knowledge that can only take shape in a relationship characterized by mutual responsiveness.[19]

Dialogical philosophers such as Søren Kierkegaard and Martin Buber can help us achieve a better understanding of the importance of the other for our own personal development. Kierkegaard spoke of the *doubly reflected communication*,[20] which uncovers these important moments of symmetry as one person facilitates the other's thinking and reflections, and where they both engage in a co-reflecting process with each other. Similarly, Buber emphasized: through the *Thou*, a person becomes an *I*.[21] From this perspective the dialogue rests on the mutual relationship, as both parties have the opportunity to understand, develop and grow in a process of giving, receiving and sharing.

Closing remarks

To conclude this chapter I would like to share a quote by William Isaacs, management consultant and a senior lecturer at MIT's Sloan School of Management, who wrote *Dialogue – the Art of Thinking Together*:

> Dialogue fulfills deeper, more widespread needs than simply "getting to yes". The aim of negotiation is to reach agreement among parties who differ. The intention of dialogue is to reach new understanding and, in doing so, to form a totally new basis from which to think and act. In dialogue, one not only solves problems, one *dis*solves them. We do not merely try to reach agreement, we try to create a context from which many new agreements might come. And we seek to uncover a base of shared meaning that can greatly help coordinate and align our actions with our values.[22]

---

19 Stelter, R. (2014). *A Guide to Third Generation Coaching.* Berlin: Springer, p. 94.
20 Kierkegaard, S. (2009). *Concluding Unscientific Postscript.* Cambridge, UK: Cambridge University Press, p. 528. (Original in Danish: *Afsluttende Uvidenskabelig Efterskrift til de Philosophiske Smuler* from 1846).
21 Buber, M. (1997). *I and Thou.* New York: Touchstone. Originally published in German in 1923.
22 Isaacs, W. (1999). *Dialogue: The Art of Thinking Together.* Strawberry Hills, NSW: Currency, p. 19.

This quote says a great deal about the ambition that the dialogue participants pursue. A dialogue is not a negotiation. There is no right or wrong. Dialogue is based on an open relationship with the other, a wondering that makes it possible to understand the other – and oneself – a little better. Dialogue is driven by a striving for insight, understanding, newness, the still-unknown, a third way – something that has the capacity to dissolve obstacles to liberation and a new openness. Dialogue requires patience, a sense of reciprocity and a lingering in something that will only be able to reveal itself in a slow and continuous exploration.

Chapter 10
Dialogue practices

Throughout the book I have sought to enhance the reader's understanding of the theoretical foundation and practical conditions of the various forms of transformative and fruitful everyday dialogues. The theory and practice presented and discussed in the book can serve as the basis of many different dialogues and professional conversations and development processes, including coaching, mentoring and other forms of transformative dialogue. I have attempted to demystify the conditions required to conduct a dialogue. The key requirement is to create a framework for the conversation and to draw up a contract that serves as the basis for everyone involved. This does not apply to ordinary everyday conversations but to dialogues with a particular development purpose. The ten 'commandments' presented in Chapter 9 will serve as the basis of the dialogue guide's ambitions and practice.

In this chapter I present examples of a dialogue practice that strives for a certain degree of depth and intensity, and which to some extent may even take place in a social context. The purpose of these examples, however, is to offer some insight into conversation practices and, hopefully, give the reader the confidence to practice this in real life. To this end, I have selected examples that in some instances include suggestions for additional reading. The examples are not meant to be analysed in depth. The knowledge imparted so far will enable the reader to make links to theoretical and practical topics that have been presented in the book.

SNAK – a card game

The first example is a social activity without any professional ambitions. *SNAK*[1] (CHAT) is a game that can bring added depth to informal talks among friends. The game was developed by Frederik Svinth and includes a deck of cards, a standard six-sided die and a rulebook. The cards can be used for familiar games,

---

1 www.snakspil.dk; until now the game is only in Danish, but there is a children's version in English: www.kickstarter.com/projects/frederiksvinth/snak-a-conversation-game-for-kids.

such as Go Fish or gin rummy. Ten special *SNAK cards* have a word printed on them (for example, 'family', 'childhood', 'crisis' or 'values'). The player who gets the card is asked to talk about the concept on the card. If the players want inspiration, they can turn to the *rulebook* and roll the *die*. For the card featuring the word 'values', for example, the rulebook lists the following questions:

- If the player rolls a 1, the rulebook suggests: 'How do you react when you meet people with different values than your own?'.
- If the player rolls a 2: 'Name three values that are close to your heart'.
- If the player rolls a 3: 'What value do you think should be common for all people?'.
- If the player rolls a 4: 'How do you live out your values?'.
- If the player rolls a 5: 'How difficult or easy do you think it is to live according to your values?'.
- If the player rolls a 6: 'What values would you like your children to remember you for?'.

I chose the 'values' card for this example, because the concept is so relevant to the context of this book. Essentially, the concepts on the special SNAK cards are intended to inspire a sort of protreptic conversation. The card game is merely intended to illustrate how an everyday social interaction can lead to a conversation that produces a different kind of sharing than a conversation about what everyone did for their summer holidays (not that that is not relevant and important too!).

Other games, such as *Hot Seat*, *Big Talk-Box*, *Table Topics* or *Therapy-The Game*, serve a similar purpose in games where everyone is a winner. The games provide a format that allows people to engage in a different way than they might normally do. The packaging for the SNAK game features a quote from a player that expresses the intention of the game: 'I have developed a closer relationship with people whom I would previously have referred to as acquaintance and who have now become good friends'. There are plenty of opportunities to improve conversations also in a private context.

Conversation salons

Andreas Lloyd and Nadja Pass are consultants with a strong social outlook. They have taken the initiative to hold a series of conversation salons throughout Denmark. With inspiration from their book, anyone can organize their own salon event.[2] The particular dialogue format they employ stems from a wish and an ambition to create a drive in social interactions by drawing the participants' attention to their desire and ability to do more than their basic civic duty. The

---

2 Lloyd, A. & Pass, N. (2015). *Samtalesaloner – Små Skub, Der Får Folk Til at Falde i Snak*. www.borgerlyst.dk. The website (partly in Danish) offers a range of ideas for establishing salons.

idea of conversation salons is not: the early café salons, Max Frisch's German book *Fragebogen*, Zeldin's *Conversation: How Talk Can Change Your Life* are important sources of inspiration. Conversation salons can help foster community spirit, civic engagement and social capital. Social capital is the glue that keeps society, organizations and communities together.[3]

In the following I present my own experience of a conversation salon that I took part in along with about 70 other participants, whom I had never met before. It was an amazing afternoon. I met wonderful, generous people who gave of themselves to each other. I still remember the event as a powerful social experience of a rare intensity.

> I became aware of the salon through an ad on borgerlyst.dk. The meeting place was a club close to a train station in central Copenhagen. It revolved around the pre-defined topic of 'drive', which would form the theme for the three-hour event on a weekday afternoon in January 2016. I arrived 15 minutes early, around 15.45. Two people, who introduced themselves as Andreas and Nadja, stood at the entrance to welcome everyone who arrived. I bought a cafe latte at the bar and looked forward to what was about to unfold. A few people were already seated in clusters of easy chairs, some on their own, others in pairs. Soon after I had arrived, Andreas came over and asked me to find someone to talk to – and with that, the event was off to a flying start. As soon as new people came in they were paired up, and each was given a note with a concept that would be one of the topics for their conversation. I was paired up with Jørgen, who was sitting at a table with a beer. Without further introduction, apart from our first names, we began to talk about our two concepts, 'choice' and 'community' which we received on our two slips of paper. We both set out talking about the associations the concept sparked for us and the stories that might be associated with it. For example, I talked about my choice of moving to Denmark, what had made me make this choice and what sort of drive lay behind this life-changing decision. We also talked about what community or sharing meant to us, including in a relationship, among friends and in the workplace. Our conversation enabled us to build a bridge between our respective perceptions. And increasingly, drive emerged as a key theme. During our conversation, which lasted about 25 minutes, Jørgen and I shared a great deal of information about ourselves. We discovered that we were more or less the same age, and that we both worked in education. However, the

continued

---

3 The concept is associated with the French philosopher Pierre Bourdieu and the American social scientist Robert Putnam, see Stelter, 2014. About social capital in organizations, see e.g. the collection of article in: Gabbay, S. M., & Leenders, R. Th. A. J (eds.) (2001). *Social Capital of Organizations (Research in the Sociology of Organizations, Volume 18)*. Bingley: Emerald Group Publishing Limited, or: Matiaske, W. (2013). *Social capital in organizations, an exchange theory approach*. Newcastle upon Tyne: Cambridge Scholars Publisher.

overriding topic that dominated our conversation was the two topics and their universal character.

After this first round, where all the participants talked about two concepts related to the concept of drive, Andreas and Nadja then welcomed everybody to the salon. There was an amazing energy in the room, an openness and an intensity that electrified the atmosphere. Nadja introduced the basic concept of the conversation salon, and Andreas described the fundamental rules – with the most important being that there has to be a clear framework guiding the process, with pre-planned questions and an underlying script.[4]

Now it was time for round two: we joined up in groups of three to four persons to discuss three questions:

- When did you last say, 'I really ought to do something!'?
- When did you last make a difference?
- How close do you have to be to someone in order to act?

The large group was now divided into many smaller groups. The noise level was high, and we huddled close together to share our stories and ideas in relation to the three questions. I found that we repeatedly engaged in general value reflections. Some of these exchanges resulted in a degree of embarrassment as one discovered that one could have easily done more in a given situation. It became clear how often we wind up in dilemma situations when we need or want to show drive.

At some point this section was interrupted. We might not have been quite done, but I had realized that I generally ought to become more involved, as an active citizen and volunteer in society, especially considering how privileged I am, in comparison to many others.

Now, Andreas stood up on a chair, so everyone could see and hear him. He kicked off another round, a so-called attitudinal barometer, sort of scaled questions for a large group.[5] People were asked to position themselves in the room depending on how they felt about the following statement: 'One person can make a big difference.' Everyone who felt the answer was predominantly yes was to move to one side of the room, while everyone who did not agree with the statement should go to the other side. When these two groups had formed, there were quite a few people in between the two positions. Next, some of the participants were asked to explain how they had come to choose their particular position.

After a short break I was then paired up with Bjarke, a young, likeable man. We were given 35 minutes to discuss three questions by interviewing each other:

---

4 A manual for the salons is found at http://samtalesaloner.dk/manual/ and described in more detail in the book mentioned above. Both are available in Danish only, but hopefully my case description will enable readers to develop their own concept for a conversation salon.
5 *Scaled Questions* is a concept known from the solution-focused approach; see more in De Jong, P. & Berg, I. K. (2002). *Interviewing for Solutions*. Belmont: Thomson.

- Who makes you want to act? What is it they do?
- Where and how did you learn to use your drive?
- How do you help others turn their ideas into reality?

After the interviews we talked together more loosely. Bjarke and I had a great talk. What stood out for me was that we had very different mindsets – probably also due to our considerable age difference, life experience and general approach to assignments. However, it was exactly this difference that made our talk so rewarding.

In the final round, I was in a group with three women. This round dealt with a dilemma that the group reflected on and sought to address. Each of us had ten minutes to present a dilemma that we felt was difficult to act on. Afterwards, the person presenting the dilemma listened, silently, to the reflections from the three listeners. This bore some similarities to the use of a reflecting team in the systemic approach and to the method of outsider witnessing (see Chapter 8).

At 19.00 this rewarding afternoon ended. I was sorry that I could not linger a little longer for a final drink. In the course of the three hours I had inspiring conversations that energized me and left me feeling engaged in a good mood. I was happy and felt tremendously enriched. All the participants had shown up with a positive attitude and the intention of having good and meaningful conversations with others about something that might ultimately make a difference to them. Everyone showed up with a desire to engage in a rewarding experience. I also realized how important the firm and kindly structure was for the positive outcome. It was Andreas and Nadja's initiative and management and the participants' engagement that created this wonderful and warm experience on a cold winter day in Copenhagen.

Group coaching of adolescent boys with a minority background

Many neighbourhoods and schools in Denmark face major social challenges, particularly in dealing with adolescent boys and young men and their ability to navigate and take responsibility for their own life. In order to generate new perspectives on these young people's lives, I initiated a research project,[6] which included offering group coaching for all the boys in grades 6 through 9 (age 13–16 years) at Rådmandsgade School in Copenhagen (a school with about 80 per cent a non-ethnic Danish origin) with the purpose of helping them to improve their coping and life skills. In the following I present a case, a brief sequence from one of my coaching sessions to illustrate how I engaged as a

---

6 The project was funded by a Nordea foundation grant and by the Danish Ministry of Cultural Affairs. Group coaching is only one element in a comprehensive two-year initiative at the school. Read more about the project at: www.holdspil.ku.dk/forskning/project4/.

coach, and how others from the group, including my co-coach in this project, Helene, acted as outsider witnesses and supportive dialogue participants.[7]

> In my coaching that day I used a rope that I laid out in a U-shape on the floor. I use the rope in an exercise that takes coaching beyond just talking. The boys engage physically. This allows for something else to happen than if they had just stay seated on their chairs. Now, Youssef was up, a charming boy with a big smile. Every time we met he greeted me with a sideways half-hug combined with a handshake. Early in the process he had already surprised me during a group session, when he acknowledged another boy in the group for his 'generosity' – amazing to see a boy of his age come up with that choice of word about a classmate. Youssef is a cheerful boy, but his self-worth and self-esteem were not always the best. He was not only the 'cool' kid; there was a vulnerability behind the cheerful face. After the end of a previous coaching session he had come up to me and hinted that he was struggling in some of his classes. He confided that he was worried that he might not be able to graduate a year and a half from then (at the time of our talk). I really appreciated the trust he showed me, but I also realized that he was not willing to disclose his doubts and insecurity publicly in a group coaching conversation.
>
> I asked Youssef what his dreams were for his life, what sort of future he was hoping for in the coming years, and I asked him to position himself alongside the rope: 'At the far left (10), if you're quite sure that you can achieve your dream, or at the far right (0), if you don't think you're going to succeed! – Or somewhere in between'. He told me that he wanted to be a soldier. I was surprised but did my best to ask follow-up questions: 'Wow! – What is it that appeals to you about being a soldier?' The other boys from the group called out: 'He wants to be a freedom fighter'. My confusion grew. Should I take this seriously? But he emphasized that they were right: 'Yes! I want to be a freedom fighter! I want to fight for what's good'.
>
> Well, that is taking a stand, I thought. I decided to engage in the conversation, although I still was not sure what to make of this information. I asked how sure he was that he could achieve this dream of becoming a soldier. And he placed himself at the far right, at zero. My confusion grew. I decided to share my doubts with him – it was hard for me to conceal it, anyway! I said to the group:
>
>> I think back to my own youth, when I was about the same age as you are now, Youssef. When I became a conscientious objector. I was very affected by the images from the Vietnam War on TV at the time. That was the first war that

---

7   The case is part of an article: Ryom, K. E., Stelter, R. & Plannthin, L. (2014). Groupcoaching og inklusion af udsatte drenge i skolen. *Kvan – et Tidsskrift for Læreruddannelsen og Folkeskolen*, 34(100), 78–90. The name in the case is anonymized.

was widely televised. I was disgusted by the way the Americans carpet-bombed the civilian population with napalm. The Americans probably sensed that the war was unwinnable. And the war had become more and more brutal. That made me decide that I would never go to war.

I was not sure if Youssef fully understood what I was talking about, but he answered, bravely: 'But I want to fight for what's good and kill the ones who are bad'. I could no longer hide my doubts, and I said: 'Well, sometimes it's hard to know who is good; both sides normally claim that they are the good guys. That is why I have decided that I want to opt for something other than weapons to resolve conflicts'.

'Well, I don't have a choice,' said Youssef, his voice rising. 'My marks aren't nearly good enough for me to get a proper education!' I wanted to comment on this surprising development in a way that allowed us to examine this new path. I tried to give him appreciative encouragement: 'I'm sure you can if you put your mind to it. That's part of the reason why Helene and I are here with you and your classmates'.

'I've got bad marks, I have no other choice. And my teacher said recently that I'm useless. I'll never get into high school!' I was shocked to hear what the teacher had said, but outwardly I tried to moderate my answer: 'If your teacher really said that, I think that's a very unfortunate comment. But sometimes teachers are stressed out too, and they may not think before they speak. But you can be certain that we have a different opinion of you!' His mates from the group supported me. One of them said, 'You just need to pay more attention in class instead of chatting so much!'

Helene made a very important contribution by reminding us all, including Youssef, of a situation in a session a few months earlier. Helene said, 'Youssef, I remember that you took extra maths classes, and you worked really hard and showed determination. Did nothing come of that?' 'Yes, in fact, I got good marks in maths'. 'You see,' we said, almost with one voice. Youssef's face lit up, and the big smile he showed so often returned. I was actually quite moved. He actually changed in this brief interchange: from feeling very low, with a sense of hopelessness, he turned his self-perception and his confidence around, from zero to a level where he began to see possibilities for himself. He was quite happy – and everybody was happy for him.

Dialogue process in a post-merger section

Some years ago, the leadership of my department at the university decided to merge two sections. As head of one of the sections, the head of department asked me to oversee the merger and head the new post-merger section. Without revealing any details about the situation in my workplace I will share information about the dialogue process, which lasted three hours and aimed to sow the seeds for a good cooperation among all the employees of the new section. About 20 of my colleagues took part in the process, which I present and describe in general terms below as a source of inspiration for others who find themselves in a similar situation (for example the need to improve cooperation in a team, to develop a common identity, to build a common culture or to explore the possibility of new join tasks). I describe the process by looking at specific tasks that I presented to facilitate the various stages of the process. The task description deviates slightly from the original as I have made it less specific.

I began the day with an introduction that outlined the purpose of the one-day event. I presented my basic ambition of ensuring that both the former sections would feel at home in the new section, and that all the employees from the two original sections would feel that they could take the best aspects of their teamwork, interests and culture with them into the new section.

Round One

Members of one of the former sections begin to talk to each other while the members of the other section listen. There is NO discussion. The members of the other group simply listen.

The conversation lasts xx minutes[8] and addresses the following questions:

- What do I appreciate most in my old team?
- What values are important for me in our teamwork?
- What is the most important thing to make room for in the new section?
- What am I going to focus on and work for in particular?

Round Two

After listening to the first group's conversation, the members of the other former section talk for xx minutes about the following questions:

- What stood out for you in the individual stories? What expression/phrase most captured your attention?
- What impression does that give you of their teamwork? What does this expression/phrase tell you about the individual member's intentions, values, beliefs, hopes and commitments?
- What does this expression/phrase tell you if you relate it to your own views and values and so forth?

---

8   If you would like to copy elements of the session, you can simply adapt the timeframe to your own specific context, whether you have a couple of hours, half a day or a full day.

- How does their story affect you on a personal level? Where does their story take you? What consequences do you draw with regard to your future cooperation? What are you most looking forward to?

In closing, the first group reflects for xx minutes based on the following questions: what are your hopes for your future cooperation? What are you most looking forward to about being part of the new, bigger section?

Now, the groups switch, so that the group that went second now speaks for xx minutes based on questions 1–4 from Round One.

Round Three, both groups combined into one

- What do I take with me from the group conversations?
- What am I most looking forward to about our future cooperation?
- What do I personally see as a new area of cooperation?
- Are there any particular tasks and strategic areas that we need to focus on more in the future?

It was important for all the participants that the final round was translated into a written document that was subsequently turned into a sort of strategy statement that everyone felt ownership of. For me, the key aspect of the process was to respect the fear of a loss of attachment, culture and good teamwork, because people were unexpectedly required to relate to a new group of people. It is important to put into words what people like and appreciate. Mutual awareness and a deeper understanding of others' and potential)common values is a requirement of a good merger process.

'Second-opinion' dialogue for improving treatments at a psychiatric centre

I asked the head of development at a psychiatric treatment centre in the Capital Region of Denmark, Nanette Forner, for permission to use the following case, which was presented in connection with an exam in the Master of Public Governance programme.[9] As head of development, Nanette continuously oversees the effort to improve the quality of patient care and treatment outcomes, in part by working with employee attitudes and values. A focus on attitudes and values clarifies the direction in the organization, and in this effort, she uses dialogue as an important tool. This requires that leadership is able 'to promote the employees'

---

9 A big thanks to my former master's student Nanette Forner for sharing this success story with the readers.

capacity for reflection and provide them with optimum conditions for development and learning'.[10] In the following I present the case, which is based on the introduction of 'second opinion', a value-based tool that incorporates the employees' and patients' experience and knowledge about how to prevent the need to use physical restraints on patients. The following text is Nanette Forner's own description of second-opinion dialogues:

> To live up to the government's goal of reducing the use of physical restraints on patients by half before 2020, the centre has established task force, made up of employees and managers, with the aim of reducing the use of restraints at the centre. The purpose of the second-opinion dialogue is to create a permanent learning and development forum, improve treatment quality, find new ways of cooperating with the patient, rethink the narrative about the patient's resources and active involvement in the treatment and identify any needs for staff training. Participants in the second-opinion process include employees who have been involved in the specific incident that involved the use of restraints, employees from other sections and functions, regular contact persons from the section and section and centre leadership.
>
> The thinking is that patients and staff have relevant knowledge and experience to help optimize treatment. To translate this knowledge and experience to learning in a forward-looking and innovative perspective it helps to facilitate it 'social discourses, actions and specific (working) relationships'.[11] Being a competent participant in second-opinion processes is therefore key to the sustainability of the changes.
>
> The leader acts as the facilitator of the second-opinion process. As facilitator, he or she has to ensure that employees and other leaders find that the dialogue takes place in an appreciative and curious atmosphere where there are no right or wrong answers. In order to generate collaborative relationships and reflections across the sections at the centre I use elements from coaching, including questions that invite outsider witnessing and move the process along. I need to introduce sufficient disruption to enable the participants to qualify their practice. I have a special responsibility to clarify the framework and my own role. I am the leader, and we are not in symmetrical relationship. My ethical stance helps shape the interaction and facilitates for the continuous organization and progress in specific collaborative processes. Because our actions reflect our values and intentions, rather than specific rules, it is important for the employees to experience that it makes a difference that they qualify each other to develop their professional and personal identity. The long-term ambition is for the employees and leaders themselves to create a space for reflecting on the use of physical restraints.

10 Stelter, R. (2014). *A Guide to Third Generation Coaching*. Berlin: Springer, p. 38.
11 Ibid., p. 111.

> ### *The head of development concludes:*
> I saw how I can use theoretical coaching concepts to qualify my own participation, as a leader, in the second-opinion process. In order to achieve our goal of user involvement and a reduction of the use of physical restraints, it is crucial to make the changes a part of the staff's thinking and everyday practice. I found that I have to act as a role model for change, that the changes have to be internalized in the organization, and that changes constitute a continuous process where the values define navigation points for the dialogue.

From my perspective I saw the case as an excellent adaptation of the dialogue approach presented in my book *A Guide to Third Generation Coaching* (2014). The initiative led to improvements in regard to the goal. At the psychiatric centre the use of physical restraints was significantly reduced. It seems justified to assume that this progress can be attributed, at least in part, to the implementation of this new understanding of the dialogue, where both the staff and the patients were positioned as co-creative experts. The key point is: development in an area requires the leader's engagement and invitation. Both are necessary for creating a space for dialogue and reflection that develops a sense of community and drive.

Closing remarks

Hopefully, the case vignettes have sufficient first-hand, experience-based substance to give you as my reader a close and intimate experience and understanding of them. I wrote or reproduced the case vignettes with two main purposes:

1. To encourage you to get started, in a personal and workplace context.
2. To clarify that it does not necessarily take extensive professional expertise to create or engage in fruitful, meaningful and transformative dialogues.

In order to create these dialogue situations, everyone involved should essentially be interested in trying something else, something that is fun, engaging and meaningful. Sometimes you need to step up and initiate a different kind of conversation. With your friends and family, you can use games, such as Hot Seat, Big Talk-Box, Table Topics, Therapy-The Game or similar conversation games. In the workplace someone in an executive position can introduce a framework for a different kind of conversation. Nanette Forner's and my own merger case may serve as examples of new ways of using dialogues in leadership. The most important condition is that everyone involved should have the *desire* and the *willingness* to try something new. It is by no means easy to initiate this type of dialogue situation. It is not always for me either. It is usually easiest in a formalized context, such as coaching or mentoring. Here, the dialogue format is fairly clear to both parties from the outset. The leader will be able to build a dialogue culture, both by acting as a good role model and by supporting initiatives for a *dialogical and transformative leadership*.[12]

---

12 Read more in Reitz, M. (2015). *Dialogue in Organizations, Developing Relational Leadership*. Houndmills, Basingstoke: Palgrave Macmillan. Or in Loon, R. (2017). *Creating Organizational Value through Dialogical Leadership, Boiling Rice in Still Water*. Dordrecht/Heidelberg/New York/London: Springer Science and Business Media Springer. Or in Hacker, S. & Roberts, Tammy. (2004). *Transformational Leadership, Creating Organizations of Meaning*. Milwaukee, WI: ASQ Quality Press.

Concluding reflections

With this book I have invited you to share a dream of improved communication, a dream of understanding and compassion, a dream of fruitful and transformative conversations that help us develop, as individuals and as communities. But it is more than a dream. It is a mission: this path towards the art of lingering in dialogue is a necessity for our well-being and quality of life, for identity development and for improving leadership and cooperation in our working life.

Although I may, at times, tend towards introversion, I too enjoy good, fruitful conversations, especially because I struggle with small talk. In professional dialogues, as a coach and mentor, I am successful. My own experience tells me that the biggest and most important precondition for succeeding in this sort of fruitful and transformative dialogue is to establish a framework for the participant's respective positions and for the ground rules. In a professional coaching conversation the context is fairly clear from the outset. Generally, transformative conversations require that the person seeking help has the desire and willingness to change. The dialogue partner who seeks support needs to trust and follow the dialogue guide, whether the guide is a coach, a co-worker, a good supervisor or a friend. The participants need to establish a trusting relationship, and that is the dialogue guide's core responsibility. Even if the conversation is fairly brief, it is important to take the time to linger.

The Greek concept of *skhole* or *scholé* can form the basis for *the art of lingering in dialogue*. *Scholé* means *intermission of work, leisure for learning, leisure, rest ease* or *idleness*.[1] The English word 'school', of course, springs from that root. *Scholé* should be viewed as a space that provides room for reflection, contemplation and lingering with another or others. This concept is contrasted by a very different concept that has not been a topic in the present book: 'negotiation', which stems from the Latin words *negotiationem* and *negotium*. These mean the opposite of the concept outlined above: a business, employment, occupation, affair.[2] The Danish leadership philosopher Michael Højlund Larsen has proposed a set of *ground rules* for *scholé*, which I reproduce here and fully second:

1 See: www.etymonline.com, look up 'school'.
2 See: www.etymonline.com, look up 'negotiation'.

- We should speak to each other with curiosity about something that matters.
- We ask questions in order to learn something – not just to find answers.
- We are not seeking to make decisions.
- We do not need to agree.
- We are not in a hurry.[3]

With this final recommendation, I send you into the real world to make your own experiences. Good intentions, having the other's best interest at heart and being on behalf of the other are the best conditions for the fruitful and transformative dialogue that I invite you to initiate.

In closing, let me repeat the motto that has guided my third-generation coaching approach throughout: *In true dialogue both sides are willing to change.*

---

[3] Michael Højlund Larsen (2012). *Dialog – en Enkel Vej til et Godt Samarbejde*. Copenhagen: L & R Business, p. 43.

References

Abramovitz, R. (2014). *Narrative Leadership: Leading with Elegance, Efficiency, and Efficacy*. Portland, OR: Sacred Circle Press.
Alexander, G. (2010). Behavioural coaching – the GROW – model. In Passmore, Jonathan. *Excellence in coaching: the industry guide* (2nd ed.). London; Philadelphia: Kogan. pp. 83–93.
Andersen, M. I. (2014). *Den Protreptiske Samtale – Din Håndbog*. [No place] Forlaget Ztrong.
Aristotle (1999). *Nicomachean Ethics* (translated by W. D. Ross). Book 1, 7; p. 10. Kitchener: Batoche Books. http://socserv.socsci.mcmaster.ca/~econ/ugcm/3ll3/aristotle/Ethics.pdf [retrieved 21 January 2016].
Bamberg, M., de Fina, A. & Schiffrin, D. (2011). Discourse and identity construction. In S. J. Schwartz *et al.* (eds.): *Handbook of Identity Theory and Research*. Dordrecht: Springer.
Bandura, A. (2012). On the functional properties of perceived self-efficacy revisited. *Journal of Management*, 38(1), 9–44.
Belk, R. W. (2013). Extended self in a digital world. *Journal of Consumer Research*, v 40, 477–500.
Bertelsen, M. & Ejlersen, S. (2005). Teamudvikling i relationen. In: R. Stelter & M. Bertelsen, (eds.): *Team – Udvikling og Læring*. Virum: Dansk Psykologisk Forlag.
Bohm, D. (1996). *On Dialogue*. New York: Routledge.
Bourdieu, P. (1990). *The Logic of Practice*. Stanford: Stanfort University Press.Boyatzis, R. E., Smith, M. L. & Beveridge, A. J. (2013). Coaching with compassion: Inspiring health, well-being and development in organizations. *Journal of Applied Behavioral Science*, 49(2), 153–178.
Brinkmann, S. (2017). *Stand Firm: Resisting the Self-improvement Craze*. Cambridge: Polity Press.
Bruner, J. (2002). *Making Stories: Law, Literature, Life*. New York, NY: Farrar, Straus and Giroux.
Buber, M. (1996). *I and Thou*. Translated by Walter Kaufmann. New York: Touchstone. (Original German edition: Ich und Du, 1923).
Cameron, M. (2014). This is common factors. *Clinical Social Work Journal*, 42, 151–160.
Charon, R. (2005). Narrative Medicine: Attention, Representation, Affiliation. *Narrative*, 13(3), 261-270. Retrieved from http://www.jstor.org/stable/2007965.
Charon, R. (2006). *Narrative Medicine: Honoring the Stories of Illness*. Oxford/New York, NY: Oxford University Press.

Cooperrider, D. L., Whitney, D. & Stavros, J. M. (2008). *Appreciative Inquiry Handbook. For Leaders of Change* (2nd edition). Brunswick, OH: Crown Custom Publishing.

Csikszentmihalyi, M. (1990). *Flow. The Psychology of Optimal Experience*. New York, NY: Harper and Row.

David, S., Clutterbuck, D. & Megginson, D. (eds.) (2013). *Beyond Goals – Effective Strategies for Coaching and Mentoring*. Farnham: Gower.

de Gennaro, I. (ed.) (2012). *Value Sources and Readings on a Key Concept of the Globalized World*. Leiden: BRILL.

de Haan, E. (2008). *Relational Coaching – Journey Towards Mastering One-to-One Learning*. Chichester: Wiley.

de Haan, E., Duckworth, A., Birch, D., Jones, C. & Lowman, R. L. (2013). Executive coaching outcome research: the contribution of common factors such as relationship, personality match, and self-efficacy. *Consulting Psychology Journal: Practice and Research*, 65(1), 40–57.

De Jong, P. & Berg, I. K. (2002). *Interviewing for Solutions*. Belmont: Thomson.

Duncan, B. (2014). *On Becoming a Better Therapist: Evidence-Based Practice One Client at a Time* (2nd edition), Chapter 1. Washington, DC: American Psychological Association.

Duncan, B. L., Miller, S. D., Wampold, B. E. & Hubble, M. A. (eds.) (2010). *The Heart & Soul of Change* (2nd edition). Washington, DC: American Psychological Association.

Ehrenberg, A. (2009). *The Weariness of the Self: Diagnosing the History of Depression in the Contemporary Age*. Montreal: McGill-Queen's University Press.

Ehrenreich, B. (2010). *Smile or Die: How Positive Thinking Fooled America and the World*. London: Granta.

Einstein, A. (2007). *The World As I See It*. San Diego, CA: The Booktree. (Original from 1953). *Mein Weltbild*. Berlin: Ullstein.

Elias, N. (2000) *The Civilizing Process*. Hoboken, NJ: John Wiley (Original German edition: *Über den Prozeß der Zivilisation*, 1939).

Elliott, R. & Greenberg, L. (2007). The essence of process-experiential/emotion-focused therapy. *American Journal of Psychotherapy*, 61(3), 241–254.

EMCC's Global Code of Ethics. www.emccouncil.org/src/ultimo/models/Download/4.pdf.

Foucault, M. (1975). *Discipline and Punishment: The Birth of the Prison*. New York: Random House. (Original French edition: Surveiller et Punir, 1975).

Frank, A. W. (1995). *The Wounded Storyteller: Body, Illness, and Ethics*. Chicago: The University of Chicago Press.

Frank, A. W. (2014). Narrative ethics as dialogical storytelling. In: *Narrative Ethics: The Role of Stories in Bioethics, Special Report, Hastings Center Report 44*, no. 1, S16–S20. DOI: 10.1002/hast.263.

Frankl, V. E. (1988). *The Will to Meaning. Foundations and Applications of Logotherapy*. New York, NY: New American Library. (Original German edition: *Der Wille zum Sinn. Ausgewählte Vorträge über Logotherapie*, 1978).

Fredslund, H. (2013). *Evaluering i et narrativt perspektiv*. Copenhagen: Dansk Psykologisk Forlag.

Freemann, A. (1994). Operative intentionality: Notes on Merleau-Ponty's approach to mental activities that are not the exclusive product of the conscious mind. *Journal of Phenomenological Research*, 24(1), 78–89.

Freeman, M. (2014). Narrative, ethics, and the development of identity. *Narrative Works: Issues, Investigations, & Interventions* 4(2), 8–27.

Gabbay, S. M., & Leenders, R. Th. A. J (eds.) (2001). *Social Capital of Organizations* (Research in the Sociology of Organizations, Volume 18). Bingley: Emerald Group Publishing Limited.
Gendlin, E. T. (1982). *Focusing*. (2nd edition). New York, NY: Bantam Books.
Gendlin, E. T. (1996). *Focusing-oriented Psychotherapy*. New York/London: The Guilford Press.
Gendlin, E. T. (1997). *Experiencing and the Creation of Meaning*. Evanston: Northwestern University Press.
Gergen, K. J. (1991). *The Saturated Self – Dilemmas of Identity in Contemporary Life*. New York: Basic Books.
Gergen, K. J. (1994). *Realities and Relationships. Soundings in Social Construction*. Boston, MA: Harvard University Press.
Gergen, K. J. (2008). *An Invitation to Social Construction* (2nd edition). London: Sage.
Gergen, K. J. (2009). *Relational Being. Beyond Self and Community*. Oxford: Oxford University Press.
Gessnitzer, S. & Kauffeld, S. (2015). The working alliance in coaching. *The Journal of Applied Behavioral Science*, 51(2), 177–197.
Giddens, A. (1984). *The Constitution of Society*. Cambridge: Polity Press.
Giddens, A. (1991). *Modernity and Self-identity. Self and Society in the Late Modern Age*. Stanford, CA: Stanford University Press.
Goffman, E. (1959). *The Presentation of Self in Everyday Life*. New York: Doubleday.
Greenberg, L. (2002). *Emotion-focused Therapy: Coaching Clients to Work Through Feelings*. Washington, DC: American Psychological Association Press.
Greenblatt, S. (1980). *Renaissance Self-Fashioning, From More to Shakespeare*. Chicago, IL: University of Chicago Press.
Gørtz, K. & Mejlhede, M. (2015). *Protreptik i Praksis – Få Væsentlige Samtaler til at Lykkes*. Copenhagen: Jurist- og Økonomforbundets Forlag.
Hacker, S. & Roberts, T. (2004). *Transformational Leadership, Creating Organizations of Meaning*. Milwaukee, WI: ASQ Quality Press.
Han, B.-C. (2015). *Burnout Society*. Stanford, CA: Stanford University.
Han, B.-C. (2015a). Pegida er et angstsymptom. *Information*, 10 February 2015. www.information.dk/523950 [accessed 1 November 2015].
Han, B.-C. (2017). *Psychopolitics. Neoliberalism and New Technologies of Power*. London; Brooklyn, NY: Verso.
Han, B.-C. (2017a). *The Scent of Time: A Philosophical Essay on the Art of Lingering*. Cambridge, UK: Polity Press.
Hanh, T. N. (2013). *The Art of Communicating*. New York: Harper Collins.
Hansen, F. T. (2012). At være i en elskende relation med verden – hvorfor ikke al filosofisk praksis kan forveksles med terapi. *Norsk Filosofisk Tidsskrift*, 47(4), 270–276.
Hansen, F. T. (2016). Socratic wonder as a way to Aletheia in qualitative research and action research. HASER. *Revista Internacional de Filosofía Aplicada*, 7, 51–88.
Hansen, J. & Henriksen, K. (2009). *Træneren som coach*. Copenhagen: Dansk Psykologisk Forlag.
Harvard Business Review (Jan–Feb 2015). The problem with authenticity: when it's OK to feel phony.
Harvey, D. (2005). *A Brief History of Neoliberalism*. Oxford: Oxford University Press.
Haslebo, G. (2004). *Relationer i Organisationer*. Virum: Dansk Psykologisk Forlag.

Haslebo, G. & Lund, G. E. (2014). *Relationsudvikling i Skolen*. Copenhagen: Dansk Psykologisk Forlag.
Heller, K. J. (1996). Power, subjectification and resistance in Foucault. *SubStance*, 25(1), 78–110.
Hühn, P., Pier, J., Schmid, W. & Schönert, J. (2009). *Handbook of Narratology* (Narratologia: Contributions to Narrative Theory/Beiträge zur Erzähltheorie). Berlin, Germany: De Gruyter.
Husserl, E. (1982). *Ideas Pertaining to a Pure Phenomenology and to a Phenomenological Philosophy – First Book: General Introduction to a Pure Phenomenology*. The Hague: Nijhoff. (Original German edition: *Ideen zu einer Reinen Phänomenologie und Phänomenologischen Philosophie*, 1913).
Ibarra, H. (2015). The authenticity paradox. *Harvard Business Review*, 93, 52–59.
Ingwersen, N. (1995). The need for narrative: The folktale as response to history. *Scandinavian Studies*, 67(1), 77–90.
Isaacs, W. (1999). *Dialogue: The Art of Thinking Together*. Strawberry Hills, NSW: Currency.
James, W. (1890). *The Principles of Psychology*. New York: Holt.
Journal of Human Values (since 1995). SAGE (http://jhv.sagepub.com/).
Kant, I. (1998). *Critique of Pure Reason*. Cambridge, UK: Cambridge University Press. (Original German edition: *Kritik der Reinen Vernunft*, 1781).
Keupp, H. & Höfer, R. (eds.) (1999). *Identitätskonstruktionen. Das Patchwork der Identitäten in der Spätmoderne*. Reinbek: Rowohlt.
Kierkegaard, S. (1992). *Either/Or. A Fragment of Life*. London: Penguin Books. (Original Danish edition: Enten – Eller, 1843).
Kirkeby, O. F. (2000). *Management Philosophy: A Radical-Normative Perspective*. Berlin/Heidelberg/New York: Springer.
Kirkeby, O. F. (2006). Coaching: For madonnaer eller ludere? *LPF-nyt om ledelse*, 9(2), 10–11.
Kirkeby, O. F., Hede, T. D., Mejlhede, M. & Larsen, J. (2008). *Protreptik – Filosofisk coaching i ledelse*. Frederiksberg: Samfundslitteratur.
Kirkeby, O. F. (2009). *The New Protreptics*. Copenhagen: CBS Press.
Kirkeby, O. F. (2016). *Protreptik – selvindsigt og samtalepraksis*. Frederiksberg: Samfundslitteratur.
Klafki, W. (2001). *Dannelsesteori og didaktik*. Århus: Klim.
Klein, O., Spears, R. & Reicher, S. (2007). Social identity performance: Extending the strategic side of SIDE. *Personality and Social Psychology Review*, 11(1), 29.
Lambert, M. J. & Barley, D. E. (2002). Research summery on therapeutic relationship and psychotherapy outcome. In: J. Norcross (ed.), *Psychotherapy Relationship That Works*, pp. 17–32. Oxford: Oxford University Press.
Lampropoulos, G. K. (2001). Common processes of change in psychotherapy and seven other social interactions. *British Journal of Guidance & Counselling*, 29(1), 21–33.
Larsen, M. H. (2012). *Dialog – en enkelt vej til et godt samarbejde*. Copenhagen: L & R Business.
Laska, K., Gurman, A., Wampold, B. & Hilsenroth, M. J. (2014). Expanding the lens of evidence-based practice in psychotherapy: A common factors perspective. *Psychotherapy*, 51(4), 467–481.
Lave, J. & Wenger, E. (1991). *Situated Learning: Legitimate Peripheral Participation*. Cambridge, UK: Cambridge University Press.

Lloyd, A. & Pass, N. (2015). *Samtalesaloner – små skub, der får folk til at falde i snak.*

Loon, R. (2017). *Creating Organizational Value through Dialogical Leadership, Boiling Rice in Still Water.* Dordrecht/Heidelberg/New York/London: Springer Science and Business Media Springer.

Lopez, S., Edwards, L. M. & Marques, S. C. (2016). *The Oxford Handbook of Positive Psychology.* Oxford: Oxford University Press.

Markus, H. & Wurf, E. (1987). The dynamic self-concept. A psychological perspective. *Annual Review of Psychology*, 38, 300.

Matiaske, W. (2013). *Social capital in organizations, an exchange theory approach.* Newcastle upon Tyne: Cambridge Scholars Publisher.

McAdams, D. P. (1993). *The Stories We Live By: Personal Myths and the Making of the Self.* New York, NY: The Guilford Press.

Mead, G. H. (2015). *Mind, Self and Society.* Chicago: University of Chicago Press.

Merleau-Ponty, M. (2012). *Phenomenology of Perception.* London: Routledge.

Miller, S., Hubble, M., & Duncan, B. (2007). *Supershrinks: What is the Secret of Their Success?* [Retrieved 12 May 2016].

Morgan, A. (2000). *What is Narrative Therapy? An Easy-to-Read Introduction.* Adelaide: Dulwich Centre.

Nesti, M. (2004). *Existential Psychology and Sport.* London: Routledge.

Nitsch, J. R. (1986). Zur handlungstheoretischen Grundlegung der Sportpsychologie. In: H. Gabler, R. Singer & J. R. Nitsch, *Einführung in die Sportpsychologie, Teil 1: Grundthemen* (pp. 188–270). Schorndorf: Hofmann.

Norcross, J. C. (2010). The therapeutic relationship. In: Duncan, B. L., Miller, S. D., Wampold, B. B. E., & Hubble, M. A., (eds.) (2010). *The Heart & Soul of Change* (2nd edition), pp. 113–141. Washington, DC: American Psychological Association.

Online Etymology Dictionary www.etymonline.com. [Accessed 29 February 2016].

Ordóñez, L. D., Schweitzer, M. E., Galinsky, A. E. & Bazerman, M. H. (2009). Goals gone wild: The systematic side effects of overprescribing goal setting. *Academy of Management Perspectives*, 23(1), 6–16.

Ørsted, C. (2013). *Livsfarlig Ledelse.* Copenhagen: People's Press.

Pihlström, S. (2010). Kant and pragmatism. *Pragmatism Today*, 1(2), 50–61.

Reitz, M. (2015). *Dialogue in Organizations, Developing Relational Leadership.* Basingstoke: Palgrave Macmillan.

Ricoeur, P. (1992). *Oneself as Another.* Chicago: University of Chicago Press.

Rogers, C. R. (1975). Empathic – An unappreciated way of being. *The Counseling Psychologist*, 5(2), 4.

Rogers, C. R. (1980). *A Way of Being.* Boston: Houghton Mifflin.

Rogers, J. (2012). *Coaching Skills.* Berkshire: Open University Press.

Rosa, H. (2018). *Resonance. A Sociology of the Relationship to the World.* Oxford: Polity Press.

Ryom, K. E., Stelter, R. & Plannthin, L. (2014). Gruppecoaching og inklusion af udsatte drenge i skolen. *Kvan. Et Tidsskrift for Læreruddannelsen og Folkeskolen*, 34(100), 78–90.

Sarbin, T. R. (ed.) (1986). *Narrative Psychology: The Storied Nature of Human Conduct.* New York, NY: Praeger.

Schau, H. J. & Gilly, M. C. (2003). We are what we post? Self-presentation in personal web space. *Journal of Consumer Research*, 30(3), 385–404.

Schilhab, T. S. S., Juelskjær, M. & Moser, T. (eds.) (2008). *The Learning Body*. Copenhagen: DPUs Forlag.

Schneeweiß, G. (2005). *Aristoteles. Protreptikos – Hinführung zur Philosophie*. Darmstadt: Wissenschaftliche Buchgemeinschaft.

Schwartz, S. H. (1992). Universals in the content and structure of values: Theoretical advances and empirical tests in twenty countries. *Advances in Experimental Social Psychology*. 25(1). San Diego, CA: Academic Press.

Schwartz, S. H. (2012). *An Overview of the Schwartz Theory of Basic Values. Online Readings in Psychology and Culture*, 2(1). http://dx.doi.org/10.9707/2307-0919.1116.

Schwartz, S. J., Luyck, K. & Vignoles, V. L. (2011). *Handbook of Identity Theory and Research*. New York, NY: Springer.

Schön, D. A. (1983). *The Reflective Practitioner. How Professionals Think in Action*. New York, NY: Basic Books.

Shotter, J. (2006). Understanding process from within: An argument for withness-thinking. *Organization Studies*, 27(5), 600.

Smith, B. & Sparkes, A. C. (2006). Narrative inquiry in psychology: Exploring the tensions within. *Qualitative Research in Psychology*, 3, 169–192.

Søltoft, P. (2008). Kierkegaard som coach. *Erhvervspsykologi*, 6(1), 2–17.

Søltoft, P. (2015). *Kunsten at Vælge Sig Selv – Om Kierkegaard, Coaching og Lederskab*. Copenhagen: Akademisk Forlag.

Sonne, M. & Tønnesvang, J. (2015). *Integrative Gestalt Practice: Transforming Our Ways of Working with People*. London: Karnacology Publications.

Stacey, R. D. (2001). *Complex Responsive Processes in Organizations: Learning and Knowledge Creation*. London: Routledge.

Stacey, R. D. (2012). Comment on debate article: Coaching psychology coming of age: The challenges we face in the messy world of complexity. *International Coaching Psychology Review*, 7(1), 91–95.

Stacey, R. D. (2012a). *The Tools and Techniques of Leadership and Management: Meeting the Challenge of Complexity*. London: Routledge.

Stelter, R. (1996). *Du Bist wie Dein Sport. Studien zur Entwicklung von Selbstkonzept und Identität*. Schorndorf: Hofmann Verlag.

Stelter, R. (1998). The body, self and identity. Personal and social constructions of the self through sport and movement (review article). *European Yearbook of Sport Psychology*, 2, 1–32.

Stelter, R. (2002). *Coaching – Læring og Udvikling*. Virum: Dansk Psykologisk Forlag.

Stelter, R. (2007). Coaching: A process of personal and social meaning making. *International Coaching Psychology Review*, 2(2), 191–201.

Stelter, R. (2008). Learning in the light of the first-person approach. In T. S. S. Schilhab, M. Juelskjær & T. Moser (eds.). *The Learning Body*. Copenhagen: Danish University School of Education Press.

Stelter, R. (2008a). Exploring body-anchored and experience-based learning in a community of practice. In T. S. S. Schilhab, M. Juelskjær & T. Moser (eds.). *The Learning Body*. Copenhagen: Danish University School of Education Press.

Stelter, R. (2008b). Approaches to enhance body-anchored learning. In T. S. S. Schilhab, M. Juelskjær & T. Moser (eds.), *The Learning Body*. Copenhagen: Danish University School of Education Press.

Stelter, R. (2009). Coaching as a reflective space in a society of growing diversity – towards a narrative, postmodern paradigm. *International Coaching Psychology Review*, 4(2), 207–217.
Stelter, R. (2010). Experience-based, body-anchored qualitative research interviewing. *Qualitative Health Research*, 20(6), 859–867.
Stelter, R. (2012). Kropslig-æstetisk læring – Teoretiske refleksioner og anvendelsesperspektiver. In Knudsen, L. E. D. (ed.). *Krop & Læring*. Copenhagen: Unge Pædagoger.
Stelter, R. (2014). *A Guide to Third Generation Coaching*. Berlin: Springer Verlag.
Stelter, R. (2014). Third generation coaching: reconstructing dialogues through collaborative practice and a focus on values. International Coaching Psychology Review, 9(1), 33–48.
Stelter, R. (2015). I tried so many diets, now I want to do it differently. – A single case study on coaching for weight loss. *International Journal of Qualitative Studies on Health and Well-Being*, 10: 26925; open access via: www.ijqhw.net/index.php/qhw/article/view/26925
Stelter, R. (2016). Sinn als Thema im Coaching. In Siegfried Greif, Heidi Möller & Wolfgang Scholl (eds.). *Handbuch Schlüsselkonzepte im Coaching*. Heidelberg: Springer.
Stelter, R. (2016a). Working with values in coaching. In T. Bachkirova, G. Spence & D. Drake (eds.), *The SAGE Handbook of Coaching*. London: Sage Publications.
Sturges, J. W. (2012). Use of therapist self-disclosure and self-involving statements. *The Behavior Therapist*, 35(5), 90–93.
Sundhedsstyrelsen. *Danskernes sundhed. Den nationale sundhedsprofil 2013*. http://sundhedsstyrelsen.dk/~/media/1529A4BCF9C64905BAC650B6C45B72A5.ashx [Retrieved 3 November 2015].
Swann, Jr., W. B. (1987). Identity negotiation: Where two roads meet. *Journal of Personality and Social Psychology*, 53, 1038–1051.
Swart, C. (2013). *Re-Authoring the World: The Narrative Lens and Practices for Organisations, Communities and Individuals*. Bryanston, JHB, South Africa: Knowledge Resources.
Urban Dictionary. JoMO, see: www.urbandictionary.com/define.php?term=jomo [Accessed 31 July 2016].
van Hauen, E. (2012). Er du autentisk? *Femina*, www.femina.dk/dit-liv/selvudvikling/er-du-autentisk [Retrieved 31 July 2016].
Vega, J. (2013). Legal rules and epieikeia in Aristotle: Post-positivism rediscovered. In: L. Huppes-Cluysenaer & N. M. M. S. Coelho (eds.). *Aristotle and the philosophy of law: Theory, Practice and Justice. Ius Gentium: Comparative Perspectives on Law and Justice 23*. Dordrecht: Springer Science+Business Media.
Wampold, B. E. (2010). The research evidence for common factors models: A historically situated perspective. In: B. L. Duncan, S. D. Miller, B. E. Wampold & M. A. Hubble (eds.), *The Heart & Soul of Change: Delivering What Works in Therapy* (2nd edition). Washington, DC: American Psychological Association.
Weick, K. E. (1979). *The Social Psychology of Organizing* (2nd edition). New York, NY: McGraw Hill.
Weick, K. E. (1995). *Sensemaking in Organisations*. Thousand Oaks, CA: Sage.
Weick, K. E. & Sutcliffe, K. M. (2015). *Managing the Unexpected* (3rd edition). San Francisco, CA: Jossey-Bass.
Wenger, E. (1998). *Communities of Practice. Learning, Meaning, and Identity*. Cambridge, UK: Cambridge University Press.

White, M. (1991). *Deconstruction Therapy*, Dulwich Centre Newsletter, 2.
White, M. (2006). *Narrativ Praksis*. Copenhagen: Hans Reitzels Forlag.
White, M. (2007). *Maps of Narrative Practice*. New York, NY: Norton.
Willig, R. (2012). Dødsstødet til new public management. *Politiken*, 22 September: http://politiken.dk/debat/kroniken/ECE1761349/doedsstoedet-til-new-public-management/ [Retrieved 1 November 2015].
Willig, R. (2013). Nu er det din egen skyld hvis livet går skævt. *Berlingske Tidende*, 12 November. www.b.dk/kultur/nu-er-det-din-egen-skyld-hvis-livet-gaar-skaevt# [Retrieved 1 November 2015].
Willig, R. (2013). *Kritikkens U-vending – en Diagnose af Forvandlingen fra Samfundskritik til Selvkritik*. Copenhagen: Hans Reitzels Forlag.
Winslade, J. & Monk, G. D. (2013). *When Stories Clash. Addressing Conflict with Narrative Mediation*. Chagrin Falls, OH: Taos Institute Publications.
Wulff, D., St. George, S., Tomm, K., Doyle, E. & Sesma, M. (2015). Unpacking the PIPs to HIPs curiosity: A narrative study. *Journal of Systemic Therapies*, 34(2), 45–58.

Websites accessed

https://en.wikipedia.org/wiki/Holacracy.
http://ing.dk/artikel/vaelg-blive-en-autentisk-leder-83638.
http://medical-dictionary.thefreedictionary.com/medical+model [Accessed 11 May 2016].
http://nexs.ku.dk/forskning/sektioner/idraet-individ-samfund/projekter/coaching/forskningsprojekter/unge-holdspil-og-medborgerskab/.
http://politiken.dk/debat/ECE2918622/pas-paa-det-perfekt-designede-menneske-er-paa-vej/ [Retrieved 10 November 2015].
http://samtalesaloner.dk/manual/.
http://socserv.socsci.mcmaster.ca/~econ/ugcm/3ll3/aristotle/Ethics.pdf [Retrieved 21 June 2016).
http://videnskab.dk/kultur-samfund/fa-et-bedre-liv-vend-selvhjaelpsbogernes-budskaber-pa-hovedet.
www.borgerlyst.dk.
www.dwds.de/.
www.dwds.de/?view=1&qu=Sinn [Retrieved 23 November 2015].
www.folkeskolen.dk/557883/naar-laererne-blander-sig-udenom-vokser-drengene.
www.focusing.org/.
www.holdspil.ku.dk/forskning/projekt4/frivillige-coaches/.
www.medborgerne.dk.
www.nexs.ku.dk/coaching.
www.protrepticus.info/protreprecon2015i20.pdf.
www.ronshoved.dk/fag/fortaellevaerksted [Retrieved 24 April 2016].
www.sageofasheville.com/pub_downloads/EMPATHIC_AN_UNAPPRECIATED_WAY_OF_BEING.pdf.
www.snakspil.dk.
www.ztrong.dk.

Index of names

Andersen, M. I. 9
Aristotle, 24, 57, 60–61, 63, 66–67, 93

Bandura, A. 63
Belk, R. W. 29
Bertelsen, M. & Ejlersen, S. 47
Bourdieu, P. 83, 125
Boyatzis, R. E., Smith, M. L. & Beveridge, A. J. 61
Brinkmann, S. 4, 30, 42
Bruner, J. 72
Buber, B. 5–6, 26, 86, 120

Charon R. 76, 98
Cooperrider, D. L. 87
Cooperrider, D. L. Whitney, D. & Stavros, J. M. 87
Csikszentmihalyi, M. 107

David, S., Clutterbuck, D. & Megginson, D. 43
de Gennaro, I. 58
de Haan, E. 112, 114
De Jong, P. & Berg, I. K. 126

Einstein, A. 46
Elias, N. 83
Elliott, R. & Greenberg, L. 90

Foucault, M. 16, 33– 35
Frank, A. W. 73
Frankl, V. E. 46–47

Freeman, M. 72
Freemann, A. 54

Gendlin, E. T. 49, 83, 119
Gergen, K. J. 25–27, 29, 32, 47, 49, 50–51, 53, 64, 91
Gessnitzer, S. & Kauffeld, S. 114
Giddens, A. 27–28, 30, 83
Goffman, E. 24, 31–32
Gørtz, K. & Mejlhede, M. 93–94
Greenberg, L. 90

Hacker, S. & Roberts, T. 134
Han, B.-C. 17–20, 29, 34–35, 57, 58
Hanh, T. N. 37, 106
Hansen, F. T. 86
Haslebo, G. 42
Hede, T. D. 90
Heidegger, M. 58
Heller, K. J. 33
Hühn, P., Pier, J., Schmid, W. & Schönert, J. 98
Husserl, E. 25

Ibarra, H. 35
Ingwersen, N. 97
Isaacs, W. 120

Kant, I. 24–26, 60–61
Keupp, H. 30
Kierkegaard, S. 4, 24, 42, 67, 72, 92, 120

Index of names

Kirkeby, O. F. 5, 13, 36, 62–67, 69, 74, 81, 89–90, 93, 118
Klein, O. 31

Lambert, M. J. & Barley, D. E. 113
Lampropoulos, G. K. 114
Larsen, J. 90
Larsen, M. H. 135–136
Laska, K., Gurman, A., Wampold, B. & Hilsenroth, M. J. 113
Lave, J. & Wenger, E. 12, 106
Lloyd, A. & Pass, N. 36, 124
Lopez, S., Edwards, L. M., Marques, S. C. 59
Loon, R. 134

McAdams, D. P. 77
McNamee, S. 117
Mead, G. H. 24, 26
Merleau-Ponty, M. 54, 75, 118
Miller, S., Hubble, M. & Duncan, B. 8, 113
Morgan, A. 98–99

Norcross, J. C. 105

Ordóñez, L. D., Schweitzer, M. E., Galinsky, A. E. & Bazerman, M. H. 43–44

Pihlström, S. 25
Putnam, R. 125
Ricoeur, P. 74

Reitz, M. 134
Rogers, C. 91, 119

Rogers, J. 67
Rosa, H. 102
Ryom, K. E., Stelter, R. & Plannthin, L. 8, 128

Sarbin, T. R. 72
Schau, H. J. & Gilly, M. C. 32
Schilhab, T. S. S., Juelskjær, M. & Moser, T. 23
Schön, D. 116
Schwartz, S. H. 62
Shotter, J. 118
Smith, B. & Sparkes, A. C. 74
Søltoft, P, 67
Sonne, M. & Tønnesvang, J. 89
Stacey, R. D. 45, 59
Stelter, R. 5, 8–9, 23, 35, 41, 43, 47–49, 51–52, 57, 75, 80, 83–84, 87, 90–91, 102, 106, 112, 116, 118, 120, 125, 132
Sturges, J. W. 105
Swann, W. B. Jr. 30
Swart, C. 103
Tomm, K. 47

Vega, J. 60

Wampold, B. 113
Weick, K. E. 13, 59
Weick, K. E. & Sutcliffe, K. M. 45
Wenger, E. 12, 106
White, M. 9, 74, 76, 102
Willig, R. 16, 59,
Wulff, D., St. George, S., Tomm, K., Doyle, E. & Sesma, M. 47

Index

acceleration 19, 20
achievement subject 17–18, 20
act-as 116
action landscape 105
affiliation 76, 77
age of marching 20
age of whizzing 20
agency 75
appreciative inquiry 87
art of lingering in dialogue 2–4, 14–15, 20, 42, 55, 57, 59, 78, 81–82, 115, 135
attention 12, 17, 19, 42, 49, 74, 76, 81–83, 88, 90–93, 95, 100, 102, 115, 124
attention to oneself 82, 88
attention triangle 82
attitudinal values 126
authenticity 34–36, 42, 80, 114

being attentive of the problem 82, 91–92
burnout society 2, 15, 17, 18, 23

capacity to act 5, 19, 30, 44–45, 62–8, 76, 93, 116
client factors 114
co-creative partner 3, 99, 101, 112
collaborative involvement 98
collective meaning-making 108
coming into contact with another 68, 88–89, 118–119
common factors 80, 111–115
communities of practice 50, 54, 106–109
concept of reflexivity 27
confidence 10, 57, 91, 123, 129

consequentialism 61
conversation salon 58, 124–126
co-reflection 45, 50, 52–53, 101, 116
co-reflective partner 45, 50, 52, 78
creative values 47
creativity 10, 90, 108, 111

deceleration 19
deconstruction 76
deconstructionist perspective 76
defining ceremonies 102
deflection 89
dialogue 111
dialogue guide 3
dialogue guide factors 114
dialogue partner 3
digital communication 23, 28, 30, 32, 41
digitization 18–19
discourse 2, 20, 23, 33–35, 43, 52–53, 74, 111
dissolution of time and space 18–19, 21, 23
dual perspective of intentionality 53
duty 60–61, 65, 124

eating disorder 33
empathy 5–6, 53, 58–59, 61, 77, 80, 88–90, 102, 105, 114, 117–119
empirical self 25, 45
epoché 25
ethics 51, 57–58, 60–61, 63, 69, 88
étos 60, 65

ētos 60, 65–66
eudaimonia 60, 64
evidence-based 112
exception question 100
excess of positivity 18
existential meaning 41–42
exoticise the familiar 76
experiential values 47
externalization 74, 92
externalizing conversation 91

Facebook 20, 28, 30
Fear of Missing Out (FoMO) 58–59
feedback-informed treatment (FIT) 116–117
fellow human companion 3–7, 46–47, 51, 60, 64, 67–68, 78, 80, 87, 101, 112
felt sense 49, 119
first-generation coaching 5, 28, 43, 45
flow 19, 49, 73, 107, 119
focussing approach 90
following and guiding 90
freedom paradox 16–17

generalized other 26
generosity 60, 128
genuine dialogue 6, 86
giving a gift 12, 104–105, 120
globalization 18, 19
goal 4–5, 14, 26, 28, 32, 35, 43–45, 57, 62–63, 65, 75, 106–107, 115, 133
group coaching 4, 127–128
GROW model 45

habits 32–33, 49, 52–54, 60, 65, 67, 83–84
habitus 83
healthy confluence 89
heteroenticity 2, 36, 42, 90, 118
hierarchy of intentionality 43, 93
human body 23, 32, 42, 54, 75, 83
humility 102
hypercomplexity 104, 71

identity formation 23–24, 29, 36
identity landscape 68, 76, 105
implicit knowledge 48

intentionality 75–76
introjection 89

joint enterprise 106–107
Joy of Missing Out (JoMO) 59

landscape of action 53, 75, *see also* action landscape
landscape of identity 53, 75, *see also* identity landscape
leadership 5, 35, 58–59, 97, 129, 131–135
learning community 12
legitimate peripheral participation 12
linear thinking in coaching 45
linger in dialogue 44
LinkedIn 28
logical cross 93–94
logical negation 94

maieutics 66–67
match, between mentor and mentee 11, 113
meaning, in an existential and phenomenological perspective 46
mentoring 11, 41, 112, 123, 134
metaphor 18, 20, 49, 75, 76, 104
moments of symmetry 45, 78, 95, 101, 105, 108, 120
mutual engagement 106
mutual relationship 77, 86, 101, 106, 111, 120
myth 76–78

narration 71
narrative 72
narrative plot 100
negotiation 30, 64, 111, 120, 121, 135
neutral facilitator 9
New Public Management 15

openness 10, 121, 126
operative intentionality 54
outside withnessing staircase 101–103

patchwork identity 30
performative self 30

personal agency 51
phrónesis 63
post-autonomy ethics 73
poststructuralist thinking 101
practical consciousness 83
practice strategies 115
present in the moment 2, 15, 19, 58, 89, 95, 113
projection 89
protreptic (perspective/approach), 44, 57, 61, 66–68, 74, 93, 95, 108, 124
psychotherapy research 113
pure ego 25, 26
purpose 6, 12,–13, 26, 44, 63, 69, 72, 75, 95, 101, 111, 115, 119, 123–124, 127, 130, 132–133

receiving a gift by listening 102
reflection-in-action 116
reflection-in-interaction 116–117
reflection-on-action 116
reframing the story 76
relational attunement 119, 120
relational competencies 80
relational factors 115
remembering 100
representation 76
resonance 102
restless nomad 32
retroflection 89

scholé 135
searching for the plot 77
second-generation coaching 6
see-as 116
self-concept 23–26, 29, 31, 34–35,
self-control 15, 17, 20–21, 34, 57, 58, 61
self-criticism 15, 16
self-exploitation 17
self-injury 33
self-management 16–17
self-monitoring 17, 20, 34, 61, 65
sense of agency 63
sense of attachment 24, 77
sensory experience 23, 41, 48, 51–52, 54, 83, 120
shared and personal learning process 10

shared meaning-making 4, 12
shared reflection 13–14, 28, 104
shared repertoire 107–108
shift in perspective 13
situational approach 67–68
situation-specific perspective 44, 57, 84
social capital 36, 97, 125
social network factors 30, 33, 114–115
stagnation 19–20
statement of position map 99, 101
striving for the ethical 92
striving for what is good 65
subjectification 33–34
supervision 80, 98
sustainable dialogue 3, 44
symmetric moment 78
symmetry in dialogue 101, 105–109

tacit knowledge 49, 83
ten 'commandments' (for coaching) 112–113, 123
thickening the story 99
third-generation coaching 2–14, 27–28, 36–37, 40–41, 45, 50, 61, 65, 75, 77, 101–106, 115, 117, 136
transcendental self 25
transformative, fruitful and genuine dialogue 6–10
translocutionarity 13, 69
trust 10, 77, 107, 113, 135
two processes of meaning-making 48–50
tyranny of positivity 59

uplifting story 100
utilitarianism 61

values 62–66
values inhabit us 63
Values-In-Action Inventory of Strength (VIA) 59
vita contemplative 57–58
volition 51–52

well-being 17, 59–61, 98, 107, 114, 135
withness-thinking 9, 52, 118–119
witnessing 7, 9, 13, 77, 102–105, 132
wondering 10, 82, 86–87, 115, 120–121

Taylor & Francis eBooks

www.taylorfrancis.com

A single destination for eBooks from Taylor & Francis with increased functionality and an improved user experience to meet the needs of our customers.

90,000+ eBooks of award-winning academic content in Humanities, Social Science, Science, Technology, Engineering, and Medical written by a global network of editors and authors.

TAYLOR & FRANCIS EBOOKS OFFERS:

- A streamlined experience for our library customers
- A single point of discovery for all of our eBook content
- Improved search and discovery of content at both book and chapter level

REQUEST A FREE TRIAL
support@taylorfrancis.com

For Product Safety Concerns and Information please contact our EU
representative GPSR@taylorandfrancis.com
Taylor & Francis Verlag GmbH, Kaufingerstraße 24, 80331 München, Germany

www.ingramcontent.com/pod-product-compliance
Lightning Source LLC
Chambersburg PA
CBHW070620300426
44113CB00010B/1593